HIGH ADVENTURE

HIGH ADVENTURE

GEORGE OTIS

FLEMING H. REVELL COMPANY
Old Tappan, New Jersey

Scripture references in this volume are from the *King James Version of the Bible.*

Poem "His Plan for Me" is from *Wings and Sky* by Martha Snell Nicholson. Copyright © 1954 Moody Press, Moody Bible Institute of Chicago. Used by permission.

Poem "Trouble Is a Servant" by John Wright Follette is used by permission of Gospel Publishing House.

ISBN 0-8007-0483-5

Copyright © 1971 by George Otis
Published by Fleming H. Revell Company
All Rights Reserved
Library of Congress Catalog Card Number: 70-169699
Printed in the United States of America

TO Dean McCullough without whom this book would never have reached print.

Contents

Foreword

Fantastic things are happening in the world market place — in the complex arena of finance, industry and commerce!

Incredible mergers, of vastly greater consequence than the blossoming Common Market, the floating mark, the fluctuating U.S. economy or the expanding trade with Red China, are shaking the board rooms of giant corporations, the seething floors of Wall Street, and thousands of smaller enterprises all over the world!

Men on every level of business are merging their assets and liabilities with the limitless resources of the living God!

Preposterous? Science-fiction? Fool's play? What's the secret?

The secret is not in learning to "use" God; it's in learning to be used *by* God (Philippians 2:12, 13). There's a vast, dynamic, soul-enriching difference. Your High Adventure will begin as you enter into your partnership with the King of Glory . . . *Eye hath not seen, nor ear heard, neither have entered into the heart of man, the things which God hath prepared for them that love him* (1 Corinthians 2:9).

A growing number of my business friends, in many fields and on every level, from corporation presidents to salesmen, are committing their careers and their lives to the God of Abraham and King David and Solomon — with spine-tingling results!

George Otis is one of these dear friends.

His is an amazing account of a dynamic, restless, successful tycoon — a man who buys and builds companies, an electronics manufacturer and business "doctor" — who realized one awful day that he was spiritually bankrupt!

The man who had built a small empire of finance and technology saw himself as a bitter failure when he added up his *spiritual* assets and liabilities. George scaled the world's mountain of success and tells in stark truth what really lies up there.

The story of how he met God, personally and in ever-deepening dimension, the almost disastrous consequences, the faith-testing decisions, and then the exhilarating, mind-bending, pulse-pounding discoveries that have tumbled one upon another since then — the ultimate in HIGH ADVENTURE.

It's adventure of the highest, deepest, widest variety; adventure with the One who spoke the worlds into existence, who numbers the hairs on our heads, who hears every prayer, who dispenses miracles and who charts the course of the planets with infinite precision.

I met George after his adventure had hit high gear, at a time when my own world started to disintegrate. The excitement in his life, the radiance in his eyes, the power in his spirit, became a lighthouse that helped steer me off the rocks of personal disaster. I believe his story will do the same for thousands — perhaps for you!

PAT BOONE

Introduction

The idea struck with such force my eyes snapped shut. A wince tightened my body. *A book?* Me write a book? Not me! What would I say? That's ridiculous!

I moved on to smother the thought with increased activity; the papers on my desk began to fly. Consciously speeding up my whole work schedule, the idea was forced back where it belonged.

At 2:15 in the afternoon the thing hit again with a walloping intrusion! I thought, "Maybe this isn't coming from inside me." Was it some external impulse? (By now I had learned— the hard way—to stop and place a call to Headquarters.)

I got up slowly from the desk, buzzed the secretary and locked my door. "Hold my calls, please." The line was clear. It always is! He's never too busy and He always seems glad to hear from me.

Folding to my knees, I called out His Name, "What is this thing that has come to me? Is it of You or is it just from my own mind? Could it be an enemy-implanted thought? Is it a delusion? I must know. I just have to know. In the Name of Jesus, dear Father, reveal to me the source and meaning of this book business, please!"

Only two minutes had gone by, and I was back pawing at the papers on the desk when David Keklikian walked in. I blurted the whole thing out to him. While David and I were sharing, Ruth and Tommy Nickel's name came to mind. I thought, "That's a good idea, I must call them."

At three earlier crossroads the Nickels (who are the publishers of *Testimony* magazine) had somehow been there to counsel me. They had either prepared me for something big looming ahead or had given some confirming word that was needed.

"Hello, Ruth, this is George. Lightning may be striking again over here in Van Nuys! We need your opinion on something." I shared everything that had been happening.

"Ruth and Tommy, you know I can't write. And even if I could, I wouldn't know what to say. There are already more good Christian books than anyone can read. Surely this idea couldn't be of God, could it?"

Then it happened. Ruth Nickel's voice rose just a little and words rolled from her lips: "In past generations I have spoken to My people through My prophets. In times before I have raised up scribes to set forth My words and My plans for the generations yet to come. Haven't I said that this present age is all but over? My Holy Word declares and present circumstances confirm that this is the last generation. I have in this hour raised up certain scribes who will write under the inspiration of My Spirit especially to this generation. This book is of Me, and My children *will* receive its message!"

What a stunning utterance! Was this a word in response to my heart cry? It had come so soon after my prayers, only hours ago, right here in my office!

Who says, "God is dead?" Here it was in the broad daylight, in a modern office setting. No hymns, no emotion—right over Mr. Bell's invention, to boot! Now it seemed we had a word from Headquarters. So—no more questions, no more problems—all we have to do now is get going, for the Lord had spoken a confirming Word through our Spirit-led friends. Right?

No, I'm afraid not. That didn't quite settle the matter. In fact, it was the very moment when the Battle of the Book *started*.

When will we ever learn that life's big warfare is really engaged in the unseen realm of the spirit world? There is constant collision in men's souls between the desires in God's heart and the forces of darkness that ever struggle against them.

Remember how God gave clear title to the land He promised to the Israelites? They had their land deed written by the finger of God Himself. Yet it was more than a generation before the Israelites acted on that deed and occupied their property. Think of it! God had already spoken the word of authority and the land belonged to them during all those years they staggered around "homeless."

Think of all those wandering years of buffeting by the adversary! The defeats, a few victories, and the lessons not learned. Remember, too, how they still had to go into their own land and *fight* with all their strength to possess what God had already given them?

They finally moved on His promise, and it was not until then that God physically wrenched the land from their enemies. Only when they acted could He fulfill in the natural realm that which He had already done in the spiritual realm.

God was ready to back His Word and their land title the very instant that He first spoke to them. To please God, it isn't enough to just *believe* Him. Obedience requires belief plus *acting* on that belief.

Within hours of God's confirming word that there would be a book, things began to happen. The attacks started from the camps of the enemy and from the camps of the flesh. It's amazing how vulnerable we can be even after a supernatural indication from God.

Quickly there set in a shower of arrows of reason militating against it. "Surely God wouldn't use you when He has such proven writers in this hour as John Sherrill, Billy Graham, Keith Miller, Gordon Lindsay, McCandlish Phillips, Dale Evans Rogers, Bob Walker, Hal Lindsay, and so many others. And these people really know how to communicate God's truths!"

Then this consideration: There really is too little to say yet from the perspective of my life. Then there were tauntings about my writing inexperience, concern that the book would be started but never finished—doubt that the first word could ever be penned, apprehension that there would never be time nor money to write it. And all of these were *valid* considerations.

Satan can even throw truth in our face to blind us. Cleverly selected tampered-with truth, but never the whole truth—never God's Truth.

Finally it was necessary (after weeks and months of these missiles) to rise up! Finally I said, "Yes, all these things are true, my enemy, but this project doesn't depend on *my* assets or abilities, but on God's. In Zechariah 4:6 it is written, . . . *Not by might, nor by power, but by my Spirit.* Didn't God even speak through a donkey?"

I threw back in his face that my God didn't need any of my meager talents or assets. He had chosen to use my weaknesses and my inability through which to express Himself. *But God hath chosen the foolish things of the world to confound the wise; and God hath chosen the weak things of the world to confound the things which are mighty* . . . (1 Corinthians 1:27). And according to this I qualified perfectly! This put the enemy to flight for a season, but he is tireless in his resistance to God's plans.

There were other near-derailments. A strange variety of fireworks exploded over the next weeks and months. First it was our company, Bible Voice. The business took off with tremendous sales breakthroughs! This put more demands on my time just to cope with the upsurge.

Then—almost as swiftly—a major business relationship breakdown struck and Bible Voice was jerked from the heights of victory down to its knees in just weeks! Suddenly we were struggling with thousands of dollars' worth of bills that had just become past due.

See it? First the overwhelming of my personal schedule by

the prosperity of Bible Voice—then the whiplash! Now there was even more of a demand on my time to wrestle with the new crises.

After some weeks all these slowly began to clear up and it was time once again to consider that book which still hung over me. We finally began some serious planning to break away to write it.

Then came the most trying assault of all. My dear wife was walking very close with the Lord, and now *she* was having some new doubts about the project. She spoke of the recent gusher of excellent books. Virginia wondered, "Perhaps this should wait until there is more for us to write." She was concerned that this might be just another idea of mine instead of a genuine leading of God.

Here it was! Virginia is the one closest to me—the one I loved and respected most—she's the only one close enough to know my *every* flaw. She was up at 5:30 every morning in the Word, and with Him in fourth-watch prayer. Virginia's reluctance toward the project just had to spark serious new questions in me, but meanwhile. . . .

The Lord was also letting tiny signals of encouragement filter through to sustain my direction. Three small books I had just written or co-authored, *Crisis-America; God, The Holy Spirit;* and *You Shall Receive Power,* were just topping 100,000 in sales. Then, Fleming H. Revell Company expressed an interest in publishing *High Adventure* without seeing the first word!

It was confusing. Reason shouted, *No.* The Spirit whispered, *Yes.* And then just when my heavy work schedule began to show patches of light ahead . . . .

It was 6:01 Tuesday morning. The big house was heaving and bucking in the torture of a killer earthquake! Tossed from bed, I began shouting a prayer: "Dear Father, in the Name of Jesus, help us!"

We felt that there wasn't a further rent made in our property from the moment that automatic prayer shot from my lips, but debris and furniture were strewn in every direction! Some of it was broken but most of it just hurled about. Concrete walls fell down as if the place had been caught in the crossfire of a tank battle. In moments the family gathered in a prayer circle. We stood and praised Him for life itself and for answered prayer.

But, as the dust was settling, I thought of it as another stroke at the book-writing schedule, and now the blows started to harden my resolve — under God — to do it! Never before had there been such a machine-gun-like series of things to discourage me from doing something that lay so heavily on my heart. Discouragement turned to encouragement. I thought, "Why, this could mean that the book might be of some value after all — otherwise it wouldn't get such attention from the adversary!"

But since Bible Voice had recently come under that financial pressure it still seemed hopeless when we thought about the expenses involved in doing the book. Then suddenly a whole series of strange things began to happen.

A phone call from a friend: "George, I want to take care of your hotel bill. Just pick the place for you and Virginia to get alone and write your new book."

Four days later Ray Barnett, a travel agent, phoned David from Canada saying, "I am sending George a round-trip ticket to Hawaii." Bob Miller (from Youth Outreach) had earlier mailed us another round-trip ticket to Hawaii. At the end of the second week, a group of men at a mountain retreat handed me $102. "This is to go toward expenses on your new book."

My dear friend and business partner, Peter Stanton, mailed a check for $200. On the stub was written, "Board of Directors' Meeting Fees." I knew, and Peter knew, what this $200 was for. Eight days later still another check from Insurance Executive Bert Fedor and Clair up in Portland. This was unprecedented!

It isn't too easy for me to receive. I guess I'm still too full of pride to be a graceful recipient, but this shower of substance was just the capper. The time to draw aside had fully come and off I went — alone — to Honolulu with my tape recorder, my Bible, and high expectations. Now I knew on whom my expectations rested!

The South Pacific morning dawned with that tropical beauty and fragrance that almost takes your breath away. I sat down on the balcony of my Hawaiian village room. There was the tape recorder, and my Bible — but my mind was utterly blank! Here came that fear again — one huge suffocating cloud of it!

The thoughts cascaded, "You will just have to go back and get to work again. This whole thing was right out of your own head. Remember those business problems needing attention back in Van Nuys? You can't do this book anyway — can't you see it now? And Virginia isn't here to type and to work with you either. Don't you remember, you really haven't got anything to say?" These were the last blows from the Satanic realm. The last flailings to stall the book.

With my hand trembling, I *forced* it to pick up the microphone and cried out for help to start! The enemy's grip was broken the very moment when, with my will, I occupied that microphone. Now the Lord could start His work in and through me. I had finally acted on His Word to me and *High Adventure* began to flow onto the tape. *My heart is inditing a good matter: I speak of the things which I have made touching on my king: my tongue is the pen of a ready writer* (Psalm 45:1).

It was only by His grace that first word was ever taped. May it somehow exalt Him! Virginia joined me at the end of that first week and the team was complete. We began.

1

The Restless Boy

The days of youth were checkered. Poets extol the wonders and joys of youth, but for me they were just irregular blobs of bittersweet.

The smell of acetone and chloroform in Dad's dental office, punctured by those occasional small cries of pain! Delight over the hand-me-down suit from a wealthy cousin—that exciting three-dollar bicycle from the old barn. (It works—grander than the first Cadillac.) Our house burning to the ground that summer night.

Memories! The glorious ritual every Christmas season—the vague outline of presents in the dark closet—sisters and brothers gathered and Dad cracking open the closet door a few inches—the five-second peek every night just before bed at the growing pile of parcels from faraway uncles and aunts. Ecstasy!

Memories! Mom and Grandfather talking about religion—one of those early Christless ministers. (A Methodist preacher who chased off to London with Eugene Debs, the militant old Socialist.) Grandpa teaching us there is no heaven or hell and explaining how we really get ours here—no sense of Christ—just sterile religious talk of theories and logic.

Thoughts of the old hard-coal stove with beauty radiating

from its hundred glorious windows when the lights were turned off—getting whipped by a boy fifteen pounds smaller and forgetting my lines in a high-school play—being captain of our football team and losing that game by my own missed tackle.

Remembrances: hoeing weeds through the Ohio cornfields for twelve-hour summer days for a whole wonderful dollar! Seeing a dead body for the first time, across the railroad tracks —the misery at school dances because of my awkwardness— that first plane ride in the open cockpit, taper-wing Waco! Sheer joy! Excitement at seeing the first Model A—that suffocating feeling of the depression and growing impatience with confinement in our little farm town.

Then a plan developed! An ancient Harley-Davidson motorcycle was found in a shed. No lights—no battery, but cheap— only ten dollars. I just had to have it and the big deal was made. A ninth grader, I went sputtering off eastward to Cape Cod—I hoped.

It was great! I slept nights on shocks of wheat and feasted from orchards. The menu was varied by an occasional candy bar or loaf of bread from a grocery. Then I saw it—the Atlantic! What a sight! The adventure germ was implanted.

Next summer—west. The Rockies were just too big for that old Harley. A quick change of plans and I was on a 12,000-horsepower steam engine, heading toward the afternoon sun between boxcars on the Nickel Plate. Then I landed on the wrong train at Hannibal and the leap ended in a long roll to the edge of the Mississippi waters. Finally there was Seattle. "Right, boy. Thirty-five cents for the room, but you must promise not to use the hot water."

Homesick and scared, I headed back immediately through the Cascades courtesy of the Great Northern. The adventurous spirit was growing! But somehow there was never a lasting satisfaction from any of it.

Then somebody told about a boy who made it to Europe hitchhiking on ships. The next summer, I thumbed to New

York with the eighty-four dollars saved up. "I'll tour Europe this summer with all that money." Up and down the docks of New York I went and then north to Boston. I talked to the ship officers of every freighter in port. "I want to work for you for nothing. Will you take me to Europe—or someplace?"

Always there was a laugh and a *no*—no takers for a kid. Then someone mentioned that freighters go all the way up the St. Lawrence to a town called Montreal. Walking and riding along the highways, I started toward Canada. Then there was another long hunt from ship to ship along the river piers, searching for the impossible.

Finally, I talked to a pink-faced Scandinavian on a rusty World War I Liberty ship *The Brandt County.* The captain looked at me in an odd way, "Son, have you any money?"

"Oh, yes."

The captain said, "Give me twenty dollars and promise not to mention it to my crew, and I'll let you work my ship to Europe. We sail for Bordeaux in the morning."

I almost tore my pocket off getting out that twenty dollars before the captain changed his mind! *The Brandt County* was a 9,000-ton vessel of Norwegian registry. On her best days she made eight knots. We sailed seventeen days through the North Atlantic ice fields. I was making beds, polishing brass, washing dishes, and scraping rust. Salty, fifteen-hour days.

Then came Bordeaux with streets full of the crippled refugees from the Spanish War. Then it was on to Belgium through the rough English Channel as the old tub groaned. At last, on a good used bike, I struck off southward from Antwerp. Pedaling and riding passenger trains I headed along the Rhine toward Heidelberg.

The German trains and streets were alive with Nazis and their war machinery. Hitler had just struck Poland! The American State Department was frantically trying to get everybody out of Germany. Somehow, it didn't all register. I didn't want to go yet—but they insisted.

Reluctantly, I pedaled back toward Antwerp to find a

freighter that would let me work my way back home. I spent
the last thirty cents in Chicago for candy bars to eat inside
the empty reefer car that would drop me off in our little town.
Again, here was that hunger for adventure followed by an
emptiness sweeping over me. Nothing quite seemed to satisfy
and nothing good was ever lasting.

Life seemed like a bundle of Roman candles that would fire
up and then leave me standing there with an empty, burned-
out, cardboard tube in my fist!

"Is this all there is to life?" More excitement had already
been packed into my young life than anyone else's in our
small town, but I was still hunting for something. Maybe I
would find it some day in college or in faraway California.
"Perhaps in Kashmir or Tahiti," I thought.

One summer I talked to our family doctor, to my wealthy
uncle, the school superintendent, and our banker friend, and
they all had the answer. They were pretty much in agreement.
It boiled down to this: Prepare yourself in school, set a lofty
target, work hard, gain a high position and you will make
money! There you'll find lasting happiness, peace, and real
satisfaction. I wanted lasting happiness more than anything.
I determined to pursue it until I owned it! But how?

There was nothing to work with—no money and no real
plan. How could a small-town boy with no connections do it?
There it was again—those little fears that always beset my
young life.

Fears! Fear of the dark and of going to bed in that faraway
upstairs room—anxiety that I couldn't make the football team.
I was afraid I'd be a coward so I guess I really was.

I was slightly sick before the kickoff of every game, but even
more afraid of being afraid! This may have motivated more
hard tackles and open field runs than if I hadn't been. Fear
tries to paralyze but at times it also motivates toward difficult
goals—like the hundred-foot water tower in our town! I was
really disturbed by heights, but more fearful, I guess, that it
would conquer me. There it stood to taunt me through the
years.

One night, the challenge of it, drove me — clutching at one rung, and then the next of the shaky ladder. Not able to look down and too terrified to look up, yet I was afraid to quit. Finally that last rung and I was up and onto the catwalk. I looked down and it almost froze me.

Now, concerned that I couldn't get down, moving fast (though nearly paralyzed) I started back.

The feeling of exhilaration with that last five-foot jump to the ground. Fear is a terrible thing when we lack that comfort from the hand of God.

And there was hesitation about starting up the success trail I had been shown — the trail up that mountain on which they assured me joy and satisfaction from high position and wealth awaited me. I felt a kind of desperation that I couldn't make it, but there was a still stronger fear not to try! Almost every teenager fights this one.

It was like that flying business. From that first ride in the taper-wing Waco, it scared me to look down, but that same feeling also stimulated every cell. It's like a roller coaster that delights you while it frightens. But, I was hooked on the clouds — the same boy that suffered on the water tower — yet I just had to fly!

I even tried to talk my instructor into just a few more hours of dual when he crawled out of that J-2 Cub yelling, "Take it around alone." I couldn't just sit there clogging up the runway, so I pushed forward the throttle and sweated! She staggered into the air and weaved around the field.

Finally, the rickety bundle of aluminum and canvas with its "Maytag" engine bounced to a horrible landing. I had done it! I had actually done it — alone!

It's a primitive feeling that lurks way down inside of us, I guess, and it feels good. Never, not even in flying the bigger, more sophisticated stuff, did I top the delight of surviving that first landing in the little Cub.

Then came the acrobatics. An instructor had taken me for a test ride and he put the craft into a couple of loops and a spin. There was that fear again, repelling, yet pulling me! Yet only months later I was doing it, strapped into the chute and pulling the nose up into a stall at 11,000 feet! I gave it hard left rudder at that last shudder of the ship. Then came that violent, blood-draining chill of a tight spin! The earth down there was turning at a dizzying speed, while the cockpit seemed to stand still. Up it came, bigger and bigger, at a heart-pounding pace! Quickly now! Wheel forward, and hard opposite rudder and she started to come out of it. Easy, and back on the wheel. Hurrah! Straight and level again at 3,000. I pushed the throttle forward for the climb back up to do it again.

But still no real satisfaction. For me they were just momentary bursts of cheap fun and thrills. Something was wrong; something was missing in my life. "Oh, well!" I told myself, "you'll find it when you get to the top of Success Mountain. Just keep driving and working and climbing and you can keep your mind numbed to God—if He exists. Fill your life with a fury of activity and force Him back! Don't even think about it." I just knew that lasting happiness was waiting for me up there at the top. Anyway, I could do it myself. Who needs God?

Meanwhile, I was still scrambling for cheap thrills. Then it was my twenty-first birthday. According to that three-score and ten formula, my life really wasn't just beginning, as people said. It was already one third *gone* and I was still totally out of synchronization with my Maker.

About then I started displaying an ornate facade. Appearing to live the fun-filled swinging life, I was really a tiny lost star wandering amongst the masses on this lonely spinning ball. There had already been thousands of miles of travel and by now hundreds of thousands of people had passed me by—but not one had yet bothered to tell the restless boy about the *Good News*.

2

Strange Harald's Saga

Gen Bredesen dying! Oh, no, surely not. What a thought! But there it was—it would come and go. I didn't even know Gen was sick, but I stopped for prayer.

Then it came. It seemed like a word of knowledge from the Lord. Yes, Gen's life was being stolen away and these things ran through my mind.

Harald is one of God's most unique children. Generous, forgetful, powerful, humorous, brilliant! A first reaction to Harald can be one of dismay at what seems like naivete. A closer look reveals it isn't that at all, but a highly evolved and potent God-dependence. His weakness is the very strength of his effectiveness in ministry for his Master.

David of old was scorned by some as he danced before the Ark, but he wasn't scorned by God to whom he was dancing in praise. Both David and Harald's uninhibited affection for God and unthrottled trust in Him gained them championship effectiveness in the all-important realm of the Spirit. Poor Harald? No, I'm afraid not! There walks one of God's richest successes—a man after God's own heart!

Who can top the miracle-strewn days and nights that run together making up a life labeled HARALD BREDESEN? Who else is sufficiently God-tuned to walk up to a dark mysterious foreign lady he had never met? While she was sitting there by a post in the lobby of the New York hotel, Harald engaged her in pleasant conversation. Minutes went by. Somehow, he moved immediately to the things that charge his soul. They talked about Jesus.

Then the young lady stiffened with amazement. Out of the mouth of this man with the turn-around collar flowed a startling cascade of sound! Then she couldn't stand it longer; her curiosity peaked.

"Where, sir, did you ever learn that? Where were you born? You don't look like an Egyptian!"

Harald stammered, "What do you mean?"

"I didn't think there was anyone left who could speak such flawless archaic Arabic. My father was an Egyptologist and he specialized in our ancient language."

Harald pleaded, "What was I saying? What was I saying?"

"Why, you know—you were speaking of the beauty and the wonder of God."

Then he told her. Harald shared how the Holy Spirit of God had spoken through his lips in a language that he had never learned, and one he didn't understand. He explained to her what had happened—right from his Bible. She was stunned!

During the next minutes she realized that God wasn't likely to squander such a remarkable miracle. Harald felt that this was God urging her to make Christ the Lord of her own life. It was then that she told him how her mother had been a Christian. She promised to go back to her people and share the Bible and this miracle with them.

(There is a new book coming that I can hardly wait to read. It's from Harald's own life adventures. I said to Harald one day, "What are you going to call your new book?"

He replied, "The second chapter of John Sherrill's book is *Harald's Strange Story*. I guess some people may think my book should be called *Strange Harald's Story!*" Actually I believe Harald's book is going to be called *The New Wineskin*.)

Back to the Gen Bredesen tragedy. Sitting out in California
on the opposite coast from the Bredesens, I had sensed somehow that Harald's tender compassion toward people was
corroding Gen's life — that their dreadful old three-story
manse hard by First Reformed Church was becoming a trap,
set and cocked by the adversary!

He was preying on Harald's total spiritual absorption and
his low level of interest in facilities and belongings. Here
was a vulnerability in Harald that the enemy was exploiting
to the destruction of his dearest Gen. I was also made aware
by the Holy Spirit of Gen's secret resentment for the old house
and the constant hoard of guests, and she was under assault
from the false accuser. The accuser was telling her that she
was just a complainer and Gen had secretly resigned herself
to this grinding existence, supposing that it was God's will
for her.

"Could these things be true?" I had no way to know all
this! Neither Harald nor Gen had spoken of them. Gen had
never even shared them with Harald. Why was I so pressed
in my spirit about something that was this delicate and intimate? It wasn't any of my business either!

The nagging persistence of the thought drove me to board
a plane for New York. How could I tell them? How should I
act? Would they receive this message?

Then the confrontation with them. The Spirit of the Lord
was gentle — so very tender with both of them. But it was true.
Why, there was a real substance to this!

Gen was weary and hurting. The Lord had spoken through
the mouth of a Californian thoughts Gen had imprisoned in
the closet of her innermost being. The message was received
by both of them.

"It's true!" they exclaimed. "It's more true than we can
ever tell you! Even so, there doesn't seem any way we can
really solve this housing problem. The manse is all our church
can afford to supply us. We can cut down on our guests, however, and we will. But we just don't have the money to buy a
house or even enough for a down payment. (You see, I was

pressing them to move from that old manse. They needed more separation from the church to cut down the parade of people running through their place, night and day.)

Harald and Gen just had to find some measure of control over their lives. They also needed to be alone more with each other, to insure spiritual and marital vitality. But—no money!

"Maybe later," they said. "We will pray about it."

Months later, Harald and I were speeding along the San Bernardino Freeway to meet Dale Evans Rogers for prayer with her mother who was over in a San Bernardino hospital. It was during one of Harald's occasional visits to minister on the West Coast. The Spirit of the Lord seemed to come on us while we were rolling through the lush groves of West Covina.

There was considerable exhortation for his inaction on their housing situation, the subject I had gone out to Mount Vernon to discuss with them! Somehow that day I had the boldness to scold Harald.

He protested, "But George, I just can't buy another house."

Then I admonished him, "Harald, how many times have I heard you minister from the pulpit for others to believe God for their needs—that He is a loving and good Father who will provide for His own!

"You are pouring out your life to minister and Christ lives within you. I think that He, too, may be tired of living in your depressing Mount Vernon place. Even if you don't have enough money, why don't you pray and ask Him for a really suitable home? Ask it for your family, for your ministry, and for Jesus to occupy with you."

Harald then described a bargain property they had recently been shown in Mount Vernon. He said that it was run-down and had been lived in by a junk-collecting recluse, but added, "We can get it cheap."

"Harald, you have set your sights too low. You have been thinking in terms of *your* resources instead of God's resources. Now think in terms of His limitless supply. Think in terms of the house that would be best for you regardless of its cost.

Think in terms of the house where Jesus, in you, would be happy to live."

Finally something was happening inside Harald. "George, you mean that I should think of the house in all of the world that I'd most love to be living in and claim it from God?"

I replied enthusiastically, "That's *exactly* what I mean! You're not the kind of person to ask the Lord for a marble palace or something ridiculous."

We were just passing a cluster of houses snuggled in the orange groves. Those low, handsome California ranch-style houses are in perhaps the $60,000 price range. Pointing, I said, "See, that house right there? Why don't you pray for something like that?"

Harald slapped his knee, shot his hand in the air, and shouted, "You asked for it, George! I'll ask for the house of my choice. I claim *your house!*"

"Wonderful, Harald!" I said and then started to laugh — but the laughter kind of froze in the air, as I weaved a bit on the road! Somehow, I knew God had heard him. Wow! He claimed our house. But quickly my logical mind got back to work and I realized that this really wasn't any threat. Harald lived 2,600 miles away and that's where his ministry was headquartered. Harald really needed to be in New York, didn't he? Anyway, even if Harald should take our house it would save us adding on as we were planning. This could be good for both of us. God does things that way!

Months and then a year went by before that phone call. Harald was coming to California again and he said, "Is the house still available?" Virginia got his room ready — the one he always liked back by the pool. Harald arrived, rushed into his room, changed to his bathing suit and — hardly stopping — jumped in the pool!

There he went, swimming on his back. Praying and singing with the Spirit. What will the neighbors think? Oh well, maybe they'll just think he's talking in some foreign language. That's not so bad, is it? Anyway it's sort of true!

Out of the pool and into his bathrobe. Immediately Harald started through the house measuring with his hands, talking to himself, "Our spinning wheel will be nice there by the fireplace. The Spanish furniture will blend with those colors in the master bedroom almost like we both planned it that way. I believe the Lord is going to act on this house matter."

"When are you coming?" I asked.

Harald's reply was, "I don't know but it could be soon."

Later that evening Harald remarked, "We've got to get down to business on this house matter. How much do you have to have for your house?" I gave him a figure.

"That seems acceptable. Last year a wealthy Christian lady in New York gave us a check that made possible our own purchase of a small house in Mount Vernon. This happened after you pressed us about living in the old manse. The small house was an interim help, but total fulfillment of my freeway claim hasn't yet been realized. We still don't have *the* house. Now perhaps it's time to lay hold of my possession. Ha!"

"Harald, even though that exhortation came through my own mouth, we will both want to get confirmation from God that He's in all this. We can't run the risk of getting you out here to the West Coast, and disrupting your ministry, unless it is His will." Harald agreed.

Over the next few months a series of occurrences happened to help Harald "try the Spirit." The Bible says, *Prove all things; hold fast that which is good* (1 Thessalonians 5:21). Soon after his California visit Harald came under conviction about his denomination's policy of baptizing infants. He laid his career and his ministry with them on the line in regard to this conflict with God's Word. The disagreement over infant baptism released him from pastoral responsibility at famous old First Reformed of Mount Vernon, N.Y. Meanwhile, the demand for Harald's speaking ministry was accelerating nationally.

He was also being pressed for ministry abroad. Then he realized that with today's near-sonic speeds it was about as feasible to headquarter in California as in New York, and that he was free to set up his household and office anywhere.

Together Harald and I structured a little spiritual test to prove this house business once and for all. We decided to "make it hard for God." Harald explained how the real estate people in Mount Vernon were telling him that houses were selling very slowly there. Further it seemed that home prices in Mount Vernon were quite depressed. I asked Harald how much he had listed his Mount Vernon house for and he told me.

I advised, "Let's do two things. First, let's set a calendar deadline—a date by which your house must be sold. The real estate people have told you that houses are moving slowly, so let's put a short four-week deadline for the Lord to bring you a sale for your present house—if you really are supposed to get our house."

For the second test, we decided to *raise* the price on Harald's house by two thousand dollars, even though the house market in Mount Vernon was poor right then. We felt that if Harald's house ever did sell under these conditions he wouldn't, in the future, ever have to question whether or not God had called him to California. He wouldn't ever have to wonder about this step even if problems might arise in the future. (This is so important on major decisions. If we make these things absolutely clear with and before the Lord, we aren't vulnerable to confusion later; otherwise we may wonder later whether we had made the decision, impulsively and "in the flesh.") Harald and I both needed a clear signal in this important decision.

Two days before our short-fused deadline, a New York man came along and bought Harald's house—and at his higher price! Harald was indeed being called by God—not just to a state or a city—but to the house on Sunnyslope. It was time for the Otises to move.

3

The House That Was Born Again

There were three specifications we brought before the Lord in our prayers after Harald claimed our Sunnyslope house. Virginia and I had asked that the Lord pick our new place, and that He give us one that would accommodate more people for home meetings.

The Sunnyslope house could only handle about sixty guests. The new wind of the Spirit now blowing is booming attendance at home meetings all over the world. Our own home had been caught up in this, and we needed more space for these meetings and for our own expanding family.

Because both our work and ministry schedule had gotten so demanding, Virginia and I had also prayed that the search for a new place be supernaturally shortened. Los Angeles is big; it is an overwhelming area that offers a confusing variety of choices. We just couldn't take the weeks and months of hunting that this would normally take. And so we started our search.

"Yes, this house is in bad shape," the realtor said, "but it has great potential! In recent years it has suffered under careless owners. It has a distinguished pedigree, but it has fallen

on very hard times. Like an elegant Vanderbilt yacht that is
now peeling and working as a humiliated garbage boat!"

The car stopped. The first glimpse just depressed me. It
was so shabby and so ragged.

"Should we go in?" The realtor asked timidly.

"Well, we might as well. We've driven all the way out
here."

Then we passed through the wide front door. All the warn-
ings and mental preparation by the realtor simply hadn't been
enough. *Nothing* could have been — it was so grim inside.
Something made me want to run; it just repulsed me! I was
too distracted by the dark atmosphere and overwhelmed by its
needs to see any potential in it.

After walking through all 5,300 feet and paying my quick
respect to its 14 rundown rooms, I said, "Let's get out of here."
But Virginia had heard from God! He had somehow revealed
that this mess was "the place." I hadn't gotten any signal at
all.

It had been built as the country estate of the famous old
Hollywood gossip columnist, Louella Parsons. Louella and
her husband, Dr. Martin, had christened it Marson's Farm
since its main house was set in its orange groves and pastures.
Clark Gable and Carole Lombard had lived here for a short
time while Gable Ranch was being completed over in Encino.
Clark planted the two beautiful olive trees that still grace its
rear yard.

Later on it was called home by the James Cagneys for some
fifteen years. It is still known as the Cagney Mansion by its
Northridge neighbors. After the Cagneys came a parade of
occupants: John Scott Trotter, musical director for Bing Crosby,
then Ruby Keeler, and others.

The white elephant later became a near wreck when turned
into a women's club. Then followed other owners, many
taking a toll and something from the great house. For a season
she had been *the* party house in the bloom of raucous Hollywood. In the estate's earlier salad years she had hosted both

the famous and the infamous, from presidents to Farouks. In the book *Tell It To Louella* we read that there were at times four hundred guests at Louella's lovely garden parties. The place had hosted everyone from Greer Garson to Errol Flynn. Both the glamorous and the foul birds had roosted here during her different eras.

No wonder the hair along my arm raised as I first walked through the place! It may have been haunted with depraved spirits of iniquity. It was as if they remained from past affairs. But Virginia's impression that this was God's choice for us remained steadfast. I had to admit it was big enough. I mean battalion-sized and just perfect for our home meetings. Then, too, it had come along quickly just as we had asked.

Now as I prayed, repulsion toward the place slowly turned to curiosity. "But how could we ever afford such a property? And how much, do you suppose, it would take to make it decent again? (Even if they gave it to us!) Could we ever clean it out? Spiritually, that is." I wasn't going to live in a house with a bunch of rusting ghosts!

A plan began to form. "How about testing this spiritually? Why don't we offer what we can afford for the estate? We could take into consideration the awful costs to make it livable as we structure our offer. We wouldn't have much to lose in making a bid that we could afford since it probably wouldn't be accepted anyway. But would it be insulting to make that kind of an offer for a place like this?"

Then an interesting idea came regarding the dark atmosphere in the main house. "Suppose this place *is* God's choice and our offer should be accepted; we could set up a tape recorder in the center of the place with amplifiers and large speakers. Then we could play our Bible tapes at high decibel level night and day for weeks before moving in."

Our bargain-basement offer on the old Victorian mansion did insult the owner just as we feared. He fumed! "Why the very idea!"

Days and then weeks went by. Finally the owner sent us a

counter offer about halfway between his price and ours. "It would be a terrific buy at this lower price! Very tempting — but nothing doing!" More days and then it happened!

The broker called us late one night and said, "Cagney Mansion is yours — and at your price. I just can't believe it! Congratulations to you both!"

Now! In with those Bible tapes and the big speakers and the Word of God boomed forth from its very center. Every atom in that house heard His Word. People going by heard it as well as every evil angel, too. The place came under the thunder and the cleansing power of it!

The whole atmosphere of the sour old place suddenly turned sweet. The place was clean and clear and full of light at last! Now even I began to get excited about the property. I thanked the Lord for Virginia's sensitivity to His leading and for her willingness to persevere in the face of my own disgust for the project.

Finally, I could see! It was obvious why nobody had wanted it. Who would ever want such a run-down depressing monstrosity? God had saved it and lowered its price for us — in His own fashion.

It was built thick and with the integrity and craftsmanship that are rare anymore. Hundreds of gallons of paint and three months of brush strokes began to change her cosmetics. Wallpaper here, a slab of marble there. New shutters. Panes of glass here. "Tear down that partition." "Replace those fixtures torn out by the souvenir hunters."

Why, it was *resurrection*. An absolute charmer! Full of light and now ringing with those Bible recordings. Just think of it: If she were in Bel Air, she would be out of sight, yet God has put her in our pocket — at His price!

The partying, the drunken laughter, and carousing to Satan's tune were stilled. That which had been used for evil was being turned to the glory of God. The praises to the Prince of Darkness were muted, and now, tonight, hundreds are singing and exalting Christ in her instead.

Across a sea of heads, the big voice boomed, "Now it's your choice. You've heard God's plan tonight. He hasn't made it hard for you. His formula is simple, but absolutely essential. No one can please the Father or come to Him through any other way. Now you are responsible for what you have heard tonight. You are without excuse and it's direct from His own Word. You've been confronted and cornered by Him. The choice is yours. He says, "If you haven't chosen Me, you've already chosen against Me. You can't stall around with this decision."

The big Texan told it like it is as he stood before the great fireplace. Two hundred and fifty-two were packed into the new-old house and they were coming under Kenneth Copeland's spiritual siege guns.

Haltingly a hand was raised over there near the piano – then that teen-ager's hand over by the window. Two more hands appeared from a couple sitting against the far wall of the Lanai room, then others, scattered here and there at the close of this home meeting.

God was moving in the place that had once been a seat of Satan during the very heyday of Hollywood. Slowly, I looked around and my heart quickened with wonder at what God had done.

The chandelier sparkled and the marble took on a new lustre. The velvet drapes and the polished wood floors seemed to assume elegance in the flow of the Spirit as God was moving.

Several months later a different hundred were sharing Christmas dinner in our new home. Dick Williams, with his guitar, was singing about the wonders of Jesus in his own unique style. Pat Boone sang "He Touched Me ' and told of his recent witness for Christ to the 23,000 students at Brigham Young University.

Then there was Albie Pearson, the Los Angeles Angels' first authentic star – the power packed little baseball player that Pat calls a "past, present, and future angel." Here was Albie thrilling us as he reported on the miraculous sweep of God's hand among the high-school kids and the Jesus people.

There they sat—bankers, a publisher, policemen, housewives, and students. Catholics, Lutherans, Baptists, Pentecostals, Methodists, Presbyterians, Church of Christ, Episcopalians, and also the unchurched. The rich and the poor, intellectuals and the uneducated. What a mixture! God's own ecumenism!

Meetings of this kind are going on all across our land today. The home meeting is God's newest phenomenon, yet it's not new at all—just a renaissance of those early Bible days when they went from house to house breaking bread, praying, and magnifying God. It's back, praise God, it's back, and it's big! There is no organization and no human promotion of home meetings. It's a spontaneous wave of God's Spirit in our times and the wave had finally broken over Marson's Farm.

That night, just as Irv Kessler the Hebrew-Christian vice-president of Liberty Records was leaving, Albie Pearson called out his name.

"Come on back, Irv. Don't leave tonight until you have met Jesus as Baptizer with the Holy Spirit. I feel that this is your time."

Somehow Irv knew and he knelt down under the chandelier. The recording executive received the Gift of the Holy Spirit right there as the baseball player laid his hands on him and prayed.

Harald's shout as we drove along that freeway had set loose forces in the spiritual realm that ultimately touched the executive there on his knees in the house that was born again!

Now it plays host to a Tuesday group of praying housewives and Virginia's Thursday Bible Class. The young teen-agers' group is Friday nights and a different gang of college-career fellows Monday nights. Special Christian guests spark unplanned meetings at Marson's Farm and God is writing by His Spirit salvation and healing, now at His Place.

"Thank you, Lord, you have answered our prayers beyond anything we could dream!"

4

Climbing Mount Babylon

The whole industrial bit began for me at Earlham College in Richmond, Indiana, when Mr. Binford, the college business manager called me out of that German class right in the middle of final exams.

He said firmly, "I can't let you finish the examinations until the rest of your second semester fee is paid."

I protested, "But, Mr. Binford, I have a job lined up for the summer building greenhouses. Can't I pay you the balance next month?"

"No, the rules say that you have to pay before the finals."

I was so embarrassed and humiliated I just picked up my books, and left the campus—a dropout. German had been difficult for me and I thought that I couldn't pass that exam after a summer lay-off.

During college I had worked nights at the Belden Cable Company in Richmond. Medical school had been my goal when I finished at Earlham. (My dad and the uncles on both sides of our family were either doctors or dentists. It was a good route that might qualify for my Mount Babylon success climb.)

At Belden I was promoted to night supervisor of my department. The manufacturing bug had bitten me. It has always thrilled me to hear big machinery running and to see new products flow down a conveyor.

One night at the diecasting machine, it hit me that making things was really fun. I was fascinated with the planning systems, the machinery, factory personnel, the lab equipment, the general rhythm of the presses — and the money. I knew then: "I'd like to do this for the rest of my life!" I was at the foot of Mount Babylon looking up.

The plant superintendent was great. I told him my idea: that I had decided to make manufacturing my life. I wanted to learn everything I could about it, and would the company consider letting me work for a few months in one department after another? I wanted to learn a little bit about every department: in maintenance, shipping, inspection, engineering, accounting, production control, purchasing, personnel, marketing, testing, and all of the production departments, too.

The superintendent replied thoughtfully, "Well, that's a new kind of a request. I'll have to think about it." Two days later, I was back in his big office, very much in awe of him. The bosses always had scared me. I didn't know where I ever got the nerve to make that request the other day.

The secretary said, "You can go in now."

There he was — all 200 pounds of him — in his expensive black suit. "Otis, I like your idea! You can start next week. You will be working for Siler first. He will work you till your tail drags! But I've told him to move you along to the next job anytime you have a feel of the one you are on."

How a kid could think of such a plan, I still don't know. After you find the Lord and spiritual eyes are opened, it is good to look back occasionally — back through the corridor of time! Sometimes you can see the places that He influenced your direction even before you ever knew Him — even to a situation here and there, where you suspect He spared your life or where He kept you from a horrible personal involvement. He may even have covered some of your sins from public gaze knowing you would — in time — become His own child.

You didn't know it then, but the Lord who knew you from the beginning of time, has always been involved in your life. He was loving you while you were still using His name as a curse!

I suspect it was so here. The Lord must have given me a little burst of wisdom. He must have fashioned this plan to get me on-the-job training — and with pay. It was a brilliant type of executive preparation that isn't available at even the best business colleges. Harvard Business School never offered a better course!

Rapidly I learned, with my hands, and through observation the real problems, tricks, and techniques of just about every facet of manufacturing. And I learned from some of the best foremen, engineers, executives, and workers all along the way. Throughout my twenty-five years in industry, those first few years provided the raw first-hand knowledge that made it difficult for my future department heads to bluff me. It was hard for them to get away with, "It can't be done." It isn't every businessman that has the privilege to work in his lifetime in every corner of his business.

After a few years it was on to Crosley which was making the secret proximity fuses and electronic communications that helped tip the scales for the Allies. Then one day came a phone call from California. A transformer plant needed a new factory superintendent. That decision took about eleven seconds! I still had that wanderlust in my blood, and I'd never seen California.

"I'll be there, in two weeks!"

As I drove through Pomona, I mused, "California sure doesn't look like I thought it would. I heard that it rained most of the time, but the hills look brown and dry. But those orange blossoms make up for a lot and the palm trees are green and graceful. The hills are high and the set of the landscape pleases me. It's exciting country for a farm boy." In ten minutes, I knew I was home!

This was Nelson Electric in Santa Monica. Art Nelson's first words to me were, "I'm sorry you came."

What a greeting!

"George, I tried to phone you in Cincinnati, but you had already left," Art told me.

I said, "What are you trying to say, Art?"

He explained, "We've had some bad setbacks here at the plant, and I just didn't want to take the responsibility of luring you all the way to the coast, and then have the business collapse under you."

Rolling up my sleeves, I worked night and day, but Nelson Electric was already a terminal case. The hole it had dug for itself was just too deep. The advances made out in the plant weren't enough to cure the ailing firm. Four months later, a big creditor blew the whistle, and she sank awkwardly right under our feet. It was a painful shock!

Sixteen-hundred miles away from all my business contacts! Two months went by as I rattled around in confusion, working as an electronics parts salesman before I got that call from my old Crosley boss, Al Hartman.

Al was now purchasing agent at a factory in Grand Rapids called Lear. I asked him to spell the name. L – E – A – R "How quick can you get to Grand Rapids?" he asked.

"Three days or less!" And I was on my way.

"So this is Lear." It was a cavernous old seven-story furniture warehouse inefficiently adapted as an electronics plant. Promotions came fast. I escalated from one little job to a medium-sized job, to a job with a bit more responsibility, and then to a good job. The pay and prestige also rose.

But I was miserable! *Now* what's wrong with me? Here I was moving up Mount Babylon so why so restless? I was homesick! – Homesick? It was a surprise discovery. How could it be? I had hardly even seen California, but there it was gnawing at me, like a haunting travelog: scenes of palm trees and orange groves, rugged mountains and rows of mansions, the blue Pacific and the hot dry sunshine. I could almost smell the flowers mixed with that salt air. I hated Grand Rapids.

It had been less than a year, but now I marched into the office of Jim Wood, the Lear plant manager.

"Jim, I'm going to leave the company. I'm sold on California, and I want to go out there and start over. I'm still young, and I've decided that I want to make my life on the West Coast."

"But George, you have a once-in-a-lifetime opportunity with us here at Lear. You have a feel for this business, and Bill respects you. I've been watching you and we are counting on you. I think you may have the stuff to carve out something good with us. It might take time for another company to spot your potential. Don't do it! Don't indulge yourself with this idea; it's too much of a luxury. The difference between Michigan and California is in your mind."

Two weeks later, I was packing, and the word had gotten to Bill Lear. He came up to the fifth floor and said, "George, I don't blame you. I've got a thing about California myself. Jim is right, the practical thing for you to do would be to stay here, but I think I understand how you feel. I don't want you to leave the company. We have an old converted dairy building in Los Angeles on Pico Boulevard. We have a dozen engineers out there working on development projects. I just called Bernie, our manager, and told him that you are coming."

I stammered, "You mean you want me to stay with Lear out there? What could I ever do for the company in that kind of a set-up?"

"Frankly, I don't know, but go on out and see if you can sweep the floors, if necessary. Maybe we'll figure out something to do in California together. Remember, I like it out there, too."

This was like Bill. Utterly unpredictable, but a prophet on occasion, too. When Bill Lear stands up, clears his throat, and announces that he's going to build a steam car and solve the world's ecology problem, I am bewildered. I may understand Bill as well as any man, but to this day I still don't know whether to roll around on the floor laughing myself sick or call my broker and say, "Buy Lear Steam stock." It's always been that way! Some of Leonardo Da Vinci's inventions never worked, but some of his other stuff was rather good

Anyway the old dairy-barn beginning developed into my role in the corporation which finally ended for me with Dick Mock's luncheon invitation. It happened this way.

"Lunch today with Dick at the Beverly Hills Hotel? Great! What time?" I pushed back the chair in my big corner office. Sitting there in our brand new factory building I thought, "Why did I say, 'Great!'?" Dick Mock, the president of Lear, and I had never hit it off too well. I always suspected it was Bill Lear who really decided a few years back to make me general manager. I sort of felt it had been done over Dick's head. Oh well, I guess it will be good to see Dick over lunch and hear what's happening at the Grand Rapids operations. . . .

During our lunch, Dick started to tell me what was on his mind. "George, I've decided to give you a new position that we have just created. You are going to become special assistant to Bill Lear and report directly to him. You will remain an officer of the corporation. I have decided to have Dr. Charles Breitwiser take over your present position as general manager. Congratulations! Bill is anxious to have you get started."

Very hot tears came to my eyes, and I blurted out, "Dick, you can't do it! We have built up this aircraft radio business that you were losing money on previously into a real profitable operation. We poured our guts into this thing. I now have almost a thousand people in my operation and our profits last month alone were seventy thousand dollars! We've made a winner of this business. Dick, you can't do it."

"George, it isn't as though we don't appreciate what you've done. You're not being fired, you know, and Bill wants a man with your decisiveness and ability. He likes to work with you and wants you now."

"Dick, don't confuse the issue, you're firing me!"

And he replied, "Well, let's face it now, George—you don't have a Doctor's degree like Chuck Breitwiser. He's new with us but he has the credentials. In the future our business will become more and more dependent on scientific minds."

I pleaded, "But Dick, have I ever had any trouble hiring scientists or Ph.D.'s? We've built a terrific staff here now, and they respect me. I have no difficulty whatsoever communicating with them, and you know, they've never been able to buffalo me in that area. Just look at our record!"

Dick was adamant, "Well, that's true, I admit, but it may not continue to work that way in years to come. And I've made up my mind."

Mount Babylon was almost scaled after all those years of the scratching, clawing climb at Lear. Now it was momentarily arrested with the firing from my exciting job. It had been eight years of constant contact with super-Bill — pure genius, eccentric, impulsive, often wrong, fun-loving, publicity-craving Bill Lear! Eight years, and I guess, I had set some kind of a new record for longevity at the top with this crazy and wonderful character.

Boy, had I ever learned a lot with him and from him! We had seen the start of the wire recorder, the tape recorder field, the executive airplane, the automatic pilot, the first good automatic direction finder, and omni-navigation. I remembered that first missile flight control system for White Sands, trips to the European air forces, Cuba, Colombia, and Canada, I'd been there as top man from Lear, and I liked it! We had assembled a crack team and steered this wobbly business into the big time in that important profit-and-loss column. We had just finished the new 70,000-foot factory at Santa Monica airport, and it had been at Lear that I found Virginia, so I felt nostalgia. But Lear was just one of the way stations on the climb toward my own golden fleece. This job had been eight years of fourteen hour days and tense six- and seven-day work weeks all jammed endlessly together. All dominated by a fearful but exciting tyrant. Yes, and there were those nerve wracking battles with Bill — and for him — alternately being bugged by and admiring the man!

Just when Bill's latest brainchild would be wrecking our whole year, there would come a flash from his brilliant mind that would produce enough products and earnings to make up for all the previous losses. What a character!

Well, it was over! "Dick, I appreciate your gentleness in telling me about this. Thank you for the offer to work with Bill on the new assignment, but I just can't do it. My pride won't let me. I'll be leaving the company."

How I missed those people over the next few weeks! I missed the company airplanes, the free car, and the salary — the prestige of being boss of a famous company. What was I going to do next?

Justin Dart phoned. He wanted to see me over at their corporate offices on LaBrea Street in Los Angeles. Rexall was starting a new medical packaging facility. Was I interested in managing it? Running a pill factory sounded deadly after Lear.

"No thanks. I guess I'll try to get started in some kind of a business of my own."

After the Rexall possibility, a real break came. Mio Illitch, president of Southwest Bank, called. "I've got a couple of fellows that want to start an electronics manufacturing business. They have the money and a beautiful building, but they need a spark plug." We made a deal within two weeks whereby I would own 25 percent of the new corporation in return for my services.

Transval Engineering Corporation had no products or people, but it had a good empty building. After about two years it was producing at a $2,300,000 rate. *Factory Magazine* did a feature article on this California plant that developed a daily profit and loss system for each production line.

Policy differences grew between the two owners and myself. I just couldn't sleep nights somehow, and announced my decision to leave. They weren't unhappy about my going. The business was booming, and they finally bought me out for cash.

Now the Otis cars were getting longer and the bank account a little fatter with each move. First the little house in Malibu, then Pacific Palisades, on to Brentwood, Beverly Hills, and finally to our hill house in Bel Air.

Now as I looked I could just barely peek over the top of the career mountain I had been climbing for oh! so long! But slowly and steadily, I had grown in iniquity! Waxing worse and worse. The sins and indiscretions which were at first hidden in my life became more open. The language became bluer. The father of a friend just couldn't rest until he had coaxed and pressured and belittled me into trying my first glass of wine. Paul was a European and he just couldn't imagine a man without a glass. He finally won, and the dependence built up slowly. There are great pressures in operating a large business. The few free hours on weekends were tackled with the same intensity for high jinx as the weekdays were for high production.

Then one day at an annual physical at a clinic, the modern hep doctor gave me a bottle of sample pills to try! "These are new," he told me. "They will give you a pickup and relax you at the same time. You can use them toward the end of the week, when you get uptight."

The next Friday night I remembered the sample pills. They were sheer magic. What a feeling! Instant vacation—at first. Later I learned their name—amphetamine (sometimes called speed)—and I was off! The combination of those pills with a drink was dynamite! These plus the supercharged work schedule accelerated my race toward the pit of Hell itself!

Here I was climbing Mount Babylon, and yet spinning out of control further and further from God. Ghastly habits picked up during this era later became the booby-trapped mine field from which Jesus Himself had to rescue me.

Along about then my friend, Phil Zonne called. "I hear you've sold out your Transval stock. If you're ready to go to work again come on over to American Electronics and help me. We have five divisions that need somebody like you to work with them. I'll give you a pretty free hand. You will need to decide whether to shut them down, sell them off, or fix them, and we can pay you well. Will you come?"

"Thanks Phil, let me think about it. I'll call you." Three

weeks later, my coat was off and my tie open. It was midnight and we were digging under rocks in one of Phil's divisions. A year later one was sold off, and one was mercifully put to sleep. Two divisions were running like Cadillacs but the fifth one was still pretty sick, and we just didn't have the heart to shut it down.

It was the Concertone Division, and I thought it had great potential. It was still losing a great amount of money every month because of weak product designs, but it did have an elegant and respected name — sort of the Bentley of tape recorders. Concertone had been the first company ever to produce stereophonic equipment for the home. (During the early years stereo was only available in theaters, so it was a technological milestone when Concertone first made a stereo recorder that could be played anywhere.)

By now my work for American except for the Concertone Division was about finished. One day Phil said, "You probably want to get back into business for yourself. Why don't you buy Concertone from us?"

"I don't know whether I want it, and I don't have enough money to buy it if I did," was my reply.

Phil volunteered, "We will sell the Concertone business to you for four hundred thousand dollars. You can take seven years to pay for it. What do you think, George?"

A call to Peter Stanton! "Peter, we have a chance to buy the Concertone tape recorder factory. I think you and I ought to team up again and build something around that business."

Pete had first been hired at Lear when we needed a crack executive assistant. Of all the candidates for the job, he had passed the UCLA battery of tests with the highest score. It wasn't just the highest score for our Lear employees — it was the highest score UCLA had ever recorded. He was a Harvard Business School graduate. Peter had the skills and now I had found the opportunity to use them.

We bought Concertone on time payment and promptly laid off everybody in the plant for three weeks. We killed every new product in the works, and I jumped on an airplane for Japan. In Tokyo we made a deal with a then little-known Japanese recorder company named TEAC run by the Tami brothers. I contracted with them to produce a tape recorder in the $600 class that would incorporate all the features that we felt Americans really wanted.

The model 505 was born while I stayed there in Japan to work with the TEAC development staff. From this Concertone shot up out of the grave and became a great name again! Soon, we incorporated as Astro-Science, and began to acquire a few other businesses and products. On the day our Astro-Science stock first sold on the open market, my personal stock holdings in the firm totaled one million, six hundred thousand dollars. It was a high water mark then. There were other business victories as well as failures: Sycan Land, Aerospace Components Corporation, Maddock, Infonics, Audio Publishers.

One weekend at the Bel Air house, it hit me. I'll never forget the moment! It was then that for the first time, I consciously realized that my fingers had clutched the top edge of that mountain I had been climbing for so long. Finally I had actually gotten a look at what lay up there!

I remembered the banker, the superintendent, our family doctor, and the uncle who had each pointed a finger toward that peak and said, "It's up there, son! If you become a success in this world, you'll be greatly rewarded. That's where you will find satisfaction, happiness, and peace!"

In a way no one ever gets to the top of that pinnacle. Nobody ever makes enough money. If you've made a million, you aren't satisfied until it's two. When you've made two, it's got to be four—but I knew that I had gotten close enough to my own childhood goal to see the real picture.

I had been tricked. It was all a ghastly lie! Here I had been captain of my ship, master of my soul. I had steered, and fought, and clawed to reach that pinnacle. And then I found it to be just a lifeless desert—a mirage—a grim void. It was shattering!

Nearly a lifetime wasted chasing after an empty dream! People would look at me and say, "There goes a lucky man, he's got it made. Respected in his field, a lovely wife, and money in the bank, an exciting life!"

Now the facade I had been presenting just collapsed before me! The chase was over and the worthless rotten prize was in my palm. I was naked, miserable, bankrupt, and empty in my soul! My pockets were full of baubles, but still that lonely emptiness inside of me. A numbing incompleteness. Something was dreadfully missing! What could it possibly be? Why, it wasn't on the Mountain of Success after all!

I had tasted of her delicacies; they were empty and bitter in my mouth. Like Solomon in Ecclesiastes 2:11, *Then I looked on all the works that my hands had wrought . . . and, behold, all was vanity and vexation of spirit.* And in 2:17 he declared, *. . . I hated life; because the work that is wrought under the sun is grievous unto me: for all is vanity and vexation of spirit.*

"What now, restless boy?"

5

God's Tender Trap

Now you know a little about my business career, but you haven't met the woman in my life who helped me find the Lord. Let's go back a few years and meet: Virginia.

My secretary at Lear blurted out one morning, "I'm getting married, Mr. Otis. We've just decided and I wanted you to know right away. My fiance doesn't want me to work, so I thought I had better give Lear a month's notice."

How inconsiderate of her! Trouble on the autopilot line, falling sales—and now this! I forced the words out, "Congratulations, Freddie. I wish you the best. Please call Personnel and ask Stan White to rush a recruiting campaign for an executive secretary."

Two weeks later, I was pushing Stan twice a day. He had only sent me second-raters—really no one worth hiring. Didn't he know Freddie would be gone in two weeks? She was gone already—in effect!

"Hello, George, I think we found your secretary." It was Stan.

"How do you know?"

"She's been working for General Telephone—still there, in fact, and they don't want to give her up. She ran the highest typing score we've seen in two years." I asked him how much experience she had, and whether she seemed to be decisive enough for the job. I needed a secretary who was able to make decisions and who could carry part of the load.

Stan said, "Well, she *is* pretty young. In fact, she's pretty, period! She seems a little quiet, and we just don't know whether you'll feel she's strong enough in this decision-making area."

"Send her up to my office and I'll try to decide whether she will do. We've let all this time get away and we can't be as choosy now. Maybe she'll work out—I hope!"

She was timid all right, but she typed like a tornado. She kept her head over that typewriter and also over our teletype link to Grand Rapids. For the next ten days I was putting out fires with both hands in the plant. Now the new VHF receiver had bugs. Two sour production lines at once! It looked like our month would be wrecked.

It was almost two weeks before I really saw her. The picture is still in my mind. She was quietly bent over that teletype machine and her fingers were moving like Cliburn's. She wore a pale pink blouse that day. Her honey-brown hair was soft and her skin had the light tan that California girls wear year 'round. She had that vitality of a very young and alive girl. Why, she was pretty! And she had that kind of wholesomeness and dignity that can challenge a fellow.

Virginia was teletyping an emergency message to Grand Rapids for me with such speed that I just talked my message through her. Then I pretty obviously stumbled as she momentarily blanked out my mind. She looked up for just a second through those incredible light blue eyes. What an effect she had on the bachelor-businessman!

Virginia is one of that rare species—a native Californian. She was born in a Presbyterian Conference grounds' cottage in the Pacific Palisades. Her father is Irish and her mom French—two people who had spent just about every Sunday of their lives in church. On my first visit the atmosphere of the Walker cottage seemed pleasant, but starkly religious.

From the time she lay helpless and protected in her mother's womb, every day and night of her life, Virginia had been the focus of prayer. And I don't mean merely someone "saying prayers." Mimi Walker is a unique woman who lives in simplicity, but who has the manner of a prophetess and a queen. When she prays, *things happen!* She has walked her life in righteousness and regular ministry to her Lord. He knew her and she knew *Him.*

At the time I first really saw Virginia at the teletype, she was in the midst of a phase some children from Christian homes experience. As her teen years wore on, she slowly began to change. A rebellion set in against what she fancied was the smothering confinement of that cottage. She became moody and then intermittently defiant. Then she entered that stage of embarrassment about her family—ashamed of their car, their home, and ashamed of her clothes.

Parents recoil in horror at the restlessness that begins to come upon teen-agers. And many times this adolescent behavior is destructive and truly dangerous. We should remember, however, that portions of the teen-age syndrome are designed by their Maker. Isn't it built into the mother eagle to finally push the growing eaglets from their nests? If young people didn't begin to yearn at some stage for life outside their own nest no new families would ever emerge among the human species!

The Walkers are modest people in a mighty wealthy area. Virginia was going to school with the Darryl Zanuck children, Elizabeth Taylor, John Derek, and a host of rich kids. Occasional visits to the homes of her friends scraped her nerves with the contrast. She had just had it and bolted from what she imagined were the bars of her religious prison. She was vulnerable! It was then that she came to Lear.

I didn't want to rush this thing, so I waited a long time—

until eleven the next morning—and poked my head out of the office. "Virginia, how about a quick sandwich up at Big Rock Restaurant?"

"Thanks, but I've got my lunch here," she said, lifting up the sack from under her desk.

"Throw it away!"

On the way up the coast, I learned a little about her situation. A businessman's work hones his ability to analyze things rapidly. He is required to make key decisions that may affect the success or failure of the business and sometimes to do it quickly. It was sort of a trademark of mine and business friends sometimes commented on this decisiveness. Plenty of times these quick-draw decisions were wrong, but I used to say this to my own management team, "It's better to make a slightly imperfect decision *fast,* than to be indecisive and allow a cancer to spread through a business while you hunt for the perfect answer. Procrastination can kill a business." I slowly developed a better blend of speed with quality after those early years.

So at 12:40, during our very first luncheon, I proposed. "Virginia, I have been hunting for you all of my life. Where have you been so long? Will you marry me?"

My decision-making speed was showing, but it took 720 times longer to get the right answer back from her!

If ever there was a case against a young Christian girl departing the protection of her family prematurely, this was it! The factories and the streets are full of characters who seek trophies of just her kind. She had promptly met a devil who would use his full arsenal of tricks, pressures, and techniques to try to rob her of her innocence.

Two years of pursuit, tenderness, arguments, temptation, victories, adventure, love, and laughter left her weak. But I hadn't counted on the supernatural. I didn't know that my premature advances were blocked, and Virginia's innocence was being guarded by the prayers of a mother way out in the Pacific Palisades!

But when both the newly divorced manager, and a playful executive began to buzz Virginia with determination, I asserted myself forcefully about this getting-married business!

Ever since that first day I really saw her I found myself wanting to be with her every free hour available to me. Some businessmen seem to have the ability to operate their plants successfully on a fifty-hour schedule. My own personal deficiencies made it necessary to pound seventy hours a week to compensate. There were no week nights or even Saturdays that I wasn't working feverishly to stay on top of the business. I seemed driven by fear of failure and of allowing my own management team to stump me.

You see, back then I was still scratching toward the top of Mount Babylon. Even when one of our suppliers would capture me for a Catalina fishing trip, I would pack along that briefcase. "I couldn't waste time on the way to the fishing banks, could I?" Papers strewn on the bunks below while the boat staggered westward through the heavy swells!

Virginia was at first exhilarated by the freedom in her new atmosphere of liberty. There was a part of her, however, that automatically held a strong cord to her past. She still had this one quirk left! Every Sunday, mind you, *every* Sunday she went to church — whether she wanted to or not. Tired from Saturday night or not, she would sit in that church balcony in a former Presbyterian church on Wilshire Boulevard that had just become independent. It served the UCLA students and the wealthy in its neighborhood. Its pastor was a highly respected Bible scholar and a fine person.

Next only to that factory, the dominating force in my life was now Virginia. And since I couldn't talk her out of it, I even started going to church on Sundays just to be with her. Another hour to hold her hand, and sense her fragrance. I was already an old thirty-four and long supercharged years had run through me and over me. Not until a few days earlier had anyone ever approached me with the big news about Jesus. Half of my life was now gone — forever. I suppose that I had skirted death several times, but still no one had ever before told me these things!

The stark memory of that has since affected my own behavior with strangers and friends. How serious it would be to know I had sat in a restaurant over a business deal, and the other person had then slipped off into oblivion without hearing this word from me either!

Yes, Virginia was "backslidden." That's the Christian technical term, isn't it? I hadn't yet learned the specialized Christian language. I felt easy in the language of my own field— accelerometers, gyros, yaw, oscilloscopes, diodes, memory banks, linear actuators, and so forth, but this Christian lingo was from a different realm.

Did you realize that Christians speak a strange language? This makes it harder for the newly interested one. He can feel left out when everyone around him is speaking it, and he doesn't really understand what they are talking about. This brings a loneliness that can make a fellow want to run.

A group of Christians will cut loose singing songs that a newcomer never heard before, and it makes him feel like he just doesn't belong. Some never have the courage to come back either.

Justification, dispensations, rapture, pretribulation, regeneration. This is sheer Greek to that new one. We mustn't jumble it all together; he isn't ready yet to hear about pretribulation or a hundred other things, until he has first met the Person of Jesus Christ. We must tell him God's simple plan for eternal life and tell it to him immediately!

Jesus made the Father's plans *simple,* and He used the language of the listener. His teaching is full of analogies about the weather, trees, crops, children, fishing, and flowers of the field. Some well-meaning Christians inadvertently confuse and complicate the Good News.

In 1 Corinthians 2 : 14 we read, *But the natural man receiveth not the things of the Spirit of God: for they are foolishness*

*unto him: neither can he know them, because they are spirit-
ually discerned.*

So there I sat in the small Westwood balcony, high above
the people reading *Factory Management* and *Aviation Week*.
I thought, "I'll sure be glad when this is over today, but it's
not all wasted. I have to keep up on my reading somewhere."
Thus it went week after week, month after month.

Working like a fiend, and living like a devil at every chance,
I said to myself, "Well, isn't this the normal way? This is the
good life isn't it? Every man does it that can afford it, doesn't
he? I'm a lot better person than Bill Jones, Charley Smith and
Frank! I never hurt anyone else with my way of life, did I?
I've never been in jail and I belong to Rotary and I'm on the
Board of Sheltered Workshop. Nobody ever sued me and I've
never sued anybody.

"I've never been caught at anything, have I? Some people
think I'm a pretty good person. I'm doing a good job for the
company and I'm making money." (Every human being ra-
tionalizes that he or she is a noble person. It is a sprout of
delusion from the father of lies himself!)

I went on daydreaming, "I guess I must be getting pretty
close to the top of my mountain now. I sure wish that Virginia wasn't so stubborn and determined! That religious
mother of hers sure gave her a lot of silly hang-ups about
living. If she weren't so pretty I'd give up on her."

"Now she's getting religion again and insists on going to
that home meeting to hear Tom Utley talk every week!" (This
was beginning to interfere with my work, and also with my
pursuit!) "She knew how much pressure there was in my job,
so why couldn't we just go park instead. Boy is she stubborn!"

Almost a year later, I was sitting in that balcony again when
my head shot up from reading *Electronics* magazine. "What
did he say down there?" It was then that I first realized that
the preaching had somehow been seeping into my ears.

Hadn't I been concentrating on my reading? Here I thought my religious hearing aid had been turned off!

Now the argumentative phase broke loose in me. At the next Utley home meeting of those religious people I finally began to talk, shooting clever (I thought) questions now and then. "How can this wonderful God shut out all those Amazon Indians that never had a chance to go to church?" You know the kind! On and on.

For the first few weeks Tom was gentle with me, but then his irritation level began to rise. Don't give up right away on someone that starts to cause trouble like this. I now know that those smart-aleck jabs heralded the very start of my real interest. Way down inside I was wanting to be convinced—I wanted them to prove to me that all this was for real. They could never have known it from my arrogant behavior, however.

Meanwhile, the Dick Mock luncheon had broken my heart and severed me from my big love—the Lear plant. For the next few weeks, my world seemed to be disintegrating all around me. Here I was slipping back just when I thought I was so near the top. In retrospect, this was just *exactly* what I needed—a fiery furnace, and a crushing blow! But how was I to know this horror was really a 24-karat prod nudging me toward God?

Now my sounding-off got even sharper in the informality of the Utley home meetings.

"Tom, how can I ever buy this thing? A baby is born in the Middle East from a mother who never had intercourse. Then this Mighty One lets a handful of soldiers beat and execute Him and now you tell me He did that on purpose. They are supposed to have buried His dead body and then a couple of days later He just comes back to life. Then He begins to walk around Jerusalem going through walls and stuff. This man stands on a hill making a speech, then like Buck Rogers, takes off into the sky."

I continued, "Tom, my business life has demanded keen

reasoning. We do our accounting by computers and our gyro tolerances must be kept to four ten-thousandths of an inch. Our financial statements are the orderly sum of all the components and they must balance out — to the penny! Everything we do in engineering and production needs to be highly tuned and logical. I can't bring myself to believe this! To me, it's like folklore that's been embellished down through generations. Didn't someone say, 'Religion is the opiate of the masses?' Tom, you're smart. How can I throw away the structure of my reasoning?"

The furnace of my life heated up another 300° centigrade over the following week. And that Sunday I sat in the balcony "reading room" beside Virginia and remembered Tom's shocking behavior. I was still mad at him! When I made my last speech he had actually taken hold of my lapel. I felt Tom wanted to shake me, but he didn't.

"George, we have heard quite enough from you! You are walking on the edge of blasphemy and it grieves my spirit. I've never said this to anyone before, but I just don't think you're going to make it. You aren't the boss in this spiritual realm, you know. You're in trouble! Your limited human logic and big ego are going to bring on your destruction. In these home classes we are dealing in the spiritual realm. Logic is a force in the natural realm, but we aren't talking about the natural — we are ministering the *super*-natural. Can't you get it through your head? This isn't a readout from a computer. It isn't a bunch of numbers to balance out either. Two and two make four will get you nowhere with God! He's not looking for brains. He *is* Wisdom, and He's not looking for your executive contribution. Who do you think manages the whole Universe? You can't do anything for Him; He wants to do something for you.

"George, you will have to put your mind on His altar. Come to Him like a trusting child in surrender — not defiance. He rightfully seeks obedience, not intellect. God understands the warring that is going on in your mind, but He's just not that hard to reach. Why don't you think about an experiment with *Him?* Just say, 'God, I don't understand this Gospel business at all, but I really do need something. If Jesus is real and if He is necessary to fill this awful empty place in my life, then I want Jesus right now!'"

Yes, I had almost gotten a look over the edge of the mountain I was trying to climb. I had felt the shock of discovering the fraud that wealth and high position bring happiness. I had been frustrated to find that material goodies aren't the answer after all. There is nothing, but nothing, on the top of that mountain! The quest for making our *own* way, and trying to be our *own* god has destroyed a billion souls. Some died on the way up and never had the chance to know of the emptiness at the top.

Now I couldn't trust my hand on the wheel of my life any longer. I had steered a true course to the port of my choice, and was shocked to learn of the bankruptcy in what man calls success. The poets say the "hounds of Hell" are pursuing men, but the loving "Hound of Heaven" patiently and persistently pursued this man.

Now his sermon was over and I heard the pastor say, "Just before we close, please bow your heads. Is there anyone here this morning that would like to ask Jesus Christ into his heart? Is there someone who wants to say, 'Yes, I want Jesus to be Lord of my life right now.' If so just raise your hand!"

A thought clutched my throat. "The experiment! Tom's experiment? Why not? What have I got to lose? I don't understand it and I guess I don't fully believe it, but maybe I can *experiment.*"

With a staggering eighth-inch step saturated with unbelief, I stabbed my hand half way up into that Westwood air, and quickly yanked it down! Nobody in that church ever saw that hand. The pastor couldn't see me. Virginia never knew it, but somewhere — eons away — Almighty God of Heaven saw it! He instantly reached down all the way and grabbed my hand. Somehow He had seen something way down deep inside me that I didn't know myself.

Like a gushing flood through my head — then through every atom of my being — my logic came unlocked and my spirit was energized! Then *I knew that I knew that I knew:* God had accepted my feeble sacrifice. I was instantly born again, made into a new creature, remanufactured, and issued new eyes to see Him that morning. The ultimate miracle! The righteous God of Heaven had in that moment taken an unrighteous, arrogant, middle-aged fraud, and breathed into him the Wind of Salvation by His Christ. God's tender trap had been fully sprung with Virginia as His bait!

His Plan for Me

When I stand at the judgment seat of Christ,
And He shows me His plan for me,
The plan of my life as it might have been,
Had He had His way — and I see . . .

How I blocked Him here, and I checked Him there,
And I would not yield my will . . .
Will there be grief in my Saviour's eyes?
Grief though He loves me still?

He would have me rich, and I stand there poor,
Stripped of all but His grace,
While memory runs like a hunted thing
Down the paths I cannot retrace.

Then my desolate heart will well-nigh break
With tears that I cannot shed;
I will cover my face with my empty hands,
I shall bow my uncrowned head . . .

Lord of the years that are left to me,
I give them to Thy hand;
Take me, break me, and mold me
To the pattern — Thou hast planned!

MARTHA SNELL NICHOLSON

6

God Drops the Other Shoe

After becoming a Christian in that old church balcony, every-thing got rosy — for a while! The pretty young secretary married the boss. In time they moved to a three-acre place in Bel Air with a long El Dorado in the carport. The swimming pool was blue and the new jobs got bigger. The bank account grew and eventually so did the family: Young George, Don, April, and Heather, and their two older sisters Kay and Markeen. Did old George straighten out, join CBMC (Christian Business Men's Committee) and live happily ever after?

Well, er, uh, not quite! I guess I must have thought salvation was instant Heaven, or at least, instant Utopia! Hadn't I been *reborn* when I accepted Christ?

The Bible says, . . . *He that believeth on the Son of God hath the witness in himself.* And the presence of Christ *was* in me and that miserable emptiness had been filled. I was har-monized with my Creator through Jesus Christ with regard to eternity. The Father saw me now through the perfection of Christ, but I didn't see me that way and neither did other people!

I now had new-creature potential, but it had to develop before it could be seen by others than the Lord. Christian character is formed by thousands of choices, and there would be an outworking of this new potential only as I would set my affections more fully on Him.

There had been sort of a picking away at trying to read the Bible before the "balcony scene," but it just seemed like a lot of confusing words and disconnected stories. Before, it was like a series of poorly told fairy tales to my dead ears.

Now, in this A.D. part of my life, I began to sense a great new love and a fascination for that Bible. It started to make a little sense to me at last. And now when I prayed, I really knew Someone was listening. That horrible blue language began to fade so that only in times of great stress did those jagged words pop out anymore. I not only continued to go to church, but now that hearing aid was turned up. I was surprised to find the words I heard were taking on new excitement!

Now the same intensity that had marked my B.C. life began to infect my Christian walk. There were also a few other changes as those fun-loving friends slipped away one by one. When I first thought about the Christian decision, I felt that if I ever went ahead it would mean great sacrifice, and that I would lose my comfortable, easy living friends. I visualized that most everything that had been occupying my nonworking hours would be spoiled if ever I became a Christian. In my mind, I weighed whether I wanted to pay such a heavy price to walk in this new arena. "Could I ever stand to move into this dull, gray, and sterile Christian world?" I hated to leave what I thought was my world of sparkling days and the nights full of kicks. But somehow, by then I already knew something was dreadfully missing in me and began to think I ought to "do my duty" and make the "sacrifice."

Wasn't that the price you had to pay to buy eternity with God? They said that, didn't they? But why didn't someone tell me about the fabulous bonuses that come along with that salvation package? I heard about the blessings in Heaven, but I wasn't prepared for His benefits while still living here on earth, too!

Everyone of the swingers that slipped out of my life over

that following year were mysteriously replaced by new Christian friends. Suddenly I discovered there were more Christians than I had ever realized, and they weren't so dull after all! A doctor here, a professor there, an engineer, an airline pilot, a nurse, the head of another plant — God's own beautiful people!

Those first two months after salvation were just great! But then it began to set in. Slowly God started to pull the props out from under me. It was time to learn to walk, and I hated it. I liked being carried around by Him and when my new-babe glow faded, I began to stagger! I had been getting into my Bible about every day now, and I was sitting under good teachings from our pastor, Tom, and several radio evangelists.

There were also helpful testimonies from men at the businessmen's meetings and occasional laymen's conventions arranged by Howard Butt. Still I knew I was slipping somehow. All those years in Egypt had infected me deeply. Throughout my life I had slowly taken on the nature of my old father, the devil. Covetousness, drunkenness, pride — these were trying to come right along into my new life to destroy it.

Then those pills brought along their own spastic mental confusions! They would rev up the thinking processes and at the same time bring on irrational judgments. Every type of dope is brewed in the worst cauldrons of hell by Satan himself! We mustn't ever be deceived that there are milder varieties that are really OK such as tranquilizers, marijuana, diet pills, and alcohol. (Yes, it, too, is a form of dope, you know.) Take it from one who has paid the price. Even so-called moderate amounts of any one of them is highly treacherous spiritually.

There seemed to be a bit of respite from these evils in my first few weeks, but now here they came again creeping back. It was ghastly! I began to pray more and with desperation! Through it all, I did manage to stay in the Word and I forced myself to listen during the week to radio teachers. But I became weary, like a worn-out swimmer about to give up as he is being swept over the falls. Something kept at me: "You will never make it. This Christian business isn't real. It's a delusion for the weak, and it's still illogical. Whatever you do don't fool *yourself*. See it doesn't work for you! You were too far gone. You're just not made for this so come back and enjoy the good life again. Don't fight it!"

Periodically, I would wonder whether there was anything further to help me out spiritually. That Bible was big! (1,265 pages of fine print). Yet I *knew* it was really God's writing and hoped that *somewhere* in it there was something I had missed that could help that sickening George Otis. Salvation had brought acute conviction to me and now I was almost suffocating in it.

From time to time I would gird my loins again and walk upright for a little while. Perhaps a stirring sermon would do it—sometimes a tiny shaft of light from my Bible. At times I didn't know where the help came from. Someone was praying for me, I guess. Occasionally I would be able to stand again for a whole week. This was maddening! I was experiencing just enough little bursts of victory to keep me staggering ahead and groping for stability in this new realm. I still didn't realize there was a raging battle taking place inside me! The forces of darkness were still contending for my soul, and my lingering sins were still giving them enough of an opening to ravish my life!

Meanwhile, the Bible teaching at my church was flowing in to me: "Jesus is coming soon. We are now in a dispensation where the Word of God is our strength. The Holy Spirit inspired the Bible and He came on the day of Pentecost to inspire those early Christians and establish the Church. There was a time when Christians prayed and mighty miracles resulted. We can read about them in that great historic Book of Acts. Those early believers went about opening blind eyes and raising the dead! People brought out their sick believing that even Peter's shadow falling on them would heal. Paul sent out handkerchiefs over which he had prayed and people were healed.

"When they praised God prison doors flew open and visions came to Peter! The ignorant fishermen became eloquent after the day of Pentecost. That little band of early Christians never had a telephone, a printed Bible, a car, a train, a radio, a tape recorder, or a printing press—yet through them, a Divine explosion turned the world upside down!

It was explained, however, that this isn't quite the pattern for Christians in our time. Those early signs and gifts were for only that time to establish the early Church. After the Bible was completed, these gifts were no longer needed. Since those early and frustrating days of my life I have often thought how much we *still* need God's Word to be *confirmed* by His wonderful works. To see the Word manifest in His mighty deeds still brings life to the Church as much as it did in A.D. 50!

During those difficult months I would sometimes wonder why God used so many pages of His Bible to tell us about all those obsolete miracles. They were really saying in our church that when John, the last apostle, died on the Isle of Patmos, God up in Heaven sort of pulled the Gifts of the Spirit switch. It was as though He had said, "These miracles, healings, and supernatural gifts of the Spirit were only for establishing the Church. They were just for the apostles and disciples to exercise." So—at John's last gasp—God pulled that *off* switch and said, "Now you don't need these anymore."

I was curious! And I guess I was even more miserable now (in some ways) than before I was saved. Now I knew how I was supposed to behave—that I was supposed to be walking in the light. I wasn't supposed to be having anything more to do with those old habits from my past.

"What's wrong with me anyway? I don't want to do these things; I hate them! Why can't I stop?" At least before my sins were cheap fun, but now salvation had taken the fun out of my sinning.

As the heat became unbearable, I started to go to Christian friends and to a pastor. It must have been sort of a lurid confession. My counselors' reactions began to form into a pattern: dismay and disappointment with me! They each used different words to advise me. Some spent a little time, and some gave a good deal of their time to discussing my problems.

The consensus of advice from my new friends went something like this: "George, I am sorry to hear you are having such a struggle with your old ways. Don't you know the answer is right there in the Word of God? Everything that man has ever encountered is covered in your Bible. Are you praying enough and are you really studying your Bible enough?" they would say, patting the Book. "No there isn't anything more for us today because there isn't anything more we need. We have it all now! You're a Christian, and you just can't do these things anymore. You've got to shape up, get into the Word more and then do what your Bible says." Still another said, "Everybody has hang-ups. Don't take your imperfections so seriously."

About once a year we would hear a fine series on error in the Church today: false teachers, false doctrines, heresy, and that these are signs of the end-times. "Watch out for people like these so-called faith healers and for those denominations where emotionalism prevails, such as those people who still believe in miracles and speaking in tongues. No one can be saved unless the Holy Spirit draws him to Christ, so we have the Holy Spirit now right here."

Meanwhile, I was still bobbing around like a porpoise, sinking under the dark waters, then shooting back up again to catch a ray of light! Spiritually unstable in all my ways, yet somehow retaining assurance of my salvation and a burning confidence in His Word—wallowing like a hog and then soaring like an eagle for a few days.

I was still making money and we were living in our Bel Air place. All the elements for a blissful life seemed available, but there was this sickness in my spirit! Never did I have the boldness to speak before a Christian group without stiffly reading every word written out ahead. Never did I have the nerve to tell anyone about Him and His plan for men and women.

I was just trying to survive, and hoping I could somehow hang on until heaven. I was trying to get through the mine field of temptation and the pits of iniquity on this earth. "Is this all there is to the Christian life? Instability and defeat? I guess I am just a no-good, rotten Christian. Surely no one else ever had these same problems."

Then came a call from Bobbi, the wife of Dr. Les Hromas! "George, could you and Virginia have dinner with Les and me at the Statler tomorrow? If you can we'd also like to have you come with us to a meeting afterward."

Dr. Hromas is an aerospace physicist with Thompson Ramo-Wooldridge Corporation. I held onto the phone and checked with Virginia, then, "Sounds great! What time did you say again? Seven o'clock tomorrow night at the Statler? We'll be there."

Dinner went by quickly and before long the four of us were edging sidewise toward four empty seats. The program had just started, and the first speaker was a Presbyterian minister in a business suit. Hadn't I seen this fellow somewhere before? He introduced himself, "My name is Dr. Glen Puder; I am pastor of Bakersfield Presbyterian Church."

"Puder? Hey! Isn't that the man we met in Luxor, Egypt at the airport? Good grief! That's a coincidence—I'd forgotten all about him." In fifteen or twenty minutes, Dr. Puder shared fascinating highlights of his own Christian life. Next an Episcopalian surgeon, Dr. William Standish Reed, gave a recitation of his own life before and after "the encounter."

At the start of the program my attitude had been pretty bad! How dare they bring us to a thing like this? It didn't take three minutes for me to see what was going on here. I had been warned about these things. But sometime during Dr. Puder's message, my fury began to soften to anger—then to confusion—and finally to curiosity.

The last speaker looked like a Catholic priest even in his dark suit and turn-around collar. What flowed from his lips, however, beat a tattoo on my soul! Never had I heard such a story! Something about this man made me sense that every impossible word he was speaking was true.

Even though I *knew* it couldn't be true, something about it rang of reality. What was it? Hadn't this all stopped after Patmos? Now be careful here. This was precisely what those warning lessons were about—so beware. "Those Pentecostals are emotional people—strong on experiences—but weak in the Word." But this was confusing!

Here was a Presbyterian with a doctor's degree in theology, and a highly educated Episcopalian surgeon who really knew his Bible—then that Dutch Reformed preacher with his degree from Lutheran Seminary.

"This doesn't fit the pattern! I wonder, could these things possibly be true?" A new quiver of hope shot through me! But I must be careful, I was in enough trouble now. The one thing that I just couldn't use more of was trouble. I had all I could handle without getting into some kind of error or cult business now. I thanked God then for the emphasis on the Word of God at my church. Now I could go and check it out knowing that my Bible would prove this or disprove it.

The pattern of all three stories that night was essentially the same. Each had come from utterly different backgrounds, and the core of their testimonies went something like this: "I accepted Christ as Saviour. Then I went to college where I walked as a Christian to the best of my ability. I tried to live the proper life, read the Bible, and go to church. While my life was vastly better than before salvation, I still lacked the ability somehow to live properly for my Creator." They described how they had staggered, and told how their lives were only a weak facsimile of those Book of Acts' Christians. They had talked about Christ and played church, but were spiritually somewhat sterile.

One after the other of these remarkable men seemed to be

telling my own story of spiritual frustration stemming from a form of godliness — but lacking living power from on high. And there I sat on the same rocks they testified of being hung up on!

Then each, in turn, recalled his own encounter with Jesus in yet another role than Saviour. They told of meeting Christ as Baptizer with the Holy Spirit and then their stories became lockstep. Each had spoken in a language he never had known. Each said he was endued with new power from on high — like all those Christians on the day of Pentecost.

I was almost afraid to let my yearnings soar for fear this would just prove false and then dash my hopes again. But then I thought, "Anyway it probably can't stand the Bible test."

Virginia was through tarrying. She had heard these things from the time she was a little girl, and knew the reality of the Spirit-filled life in others. She had been prepared from her youth for just such a time as this. Now she was ready — actually overripe!

She had been bushwhacked by the intrusion into her life by my own sinful person. By that night she had had quite enough of our living on the wrong side of God's tracks. God instantly triggered something in her! There was a determination to seek this gift of God she had known about since a child. Virginia met Christ as Baptizer with the Holy Ghost that very night and just like on the day of Pentecost — He gave her a beautiful new language right on the spot.

Virginia was never quite the same again. It was instant liberty and a fresh loveliness from her new completeness in Christ!

We drove home that night chattering ninety-miles-an-hour like a couple of jaybirds. Something incredible had happened to my girl! I knew her as no other person alive did, and now she was different, and I liked it — I liked it! And yet I felt *left out.*

7

Moment of Truth

There was a new fragrance in Virginia all that next week. There had always been a hint of stiffness there stemming, perhaps, from some inferiority complex — maybe from her girlhood. Even when she was outgoing, it seemed a bit forced somehow; her personality was slightly ingrown.

Now she was like instant sunshine! It was as though a moist tropical breeze had touched a spring bud. She opened up into full flower, right before my eyes! Why, I never saw anything like it in my life! She was more attractive somehow, more affectionate, and more poised, too.

It was a Tuesday morning and the sun was bright through my office window at the El Monte plant. I had paused to wonder at the change in Virginia (and I was still feeling left out) as I began to talk to Him.

"Dear Heavenly Father, what does this Holy Ghost business mean? My spirit seems divided. Have the pressures here at Astro-Science unbalanced my emotions? What about those things I heard from Puder, Bredesen and Dr. Reed? Were they lying — or are they under some spirit of deception? Protect me, please, if this baptism isn't for our day. It seems like ever since I first met You I've heard cautions about the

Pentecostals. Was that You protecting me? My old Bible teachers are mature Christians, and they've studied for so much longer than I. But what about Virginia? Something really has happened there—something very beautiful! Surely Satan wouldn't have uncorked that bottle of praise in her. She never praised You like that before! That couldn't be satanic—but then, what is it? I am such a mess—such a failure as a Christian and as a person. How can I sort these things out? Somehow, give me a plan that I might know *for sure* whether this Baptism with the Holy Spirit is of You or not. Don't let me follow some spirit of delusion now just because of my own personal needs at this stage. Where shall I start? Whom shall I ask about this? Help me, dear Father, in the name of Jesus, I ask this."

I opened my eyes and rolled back the swivel chair folding my hands behind my head and just stared at the paneled walls for a minute. Our El Monte facility was big! Two hundred thousand square feet in a sprawled complex of buildings—two hundred thousand feet of trouble!

The climate control system for the Vandenberg Minute Man instrumentation was four-and-one-half weeks behind schedule and already $130,000 over budget. One of the executives was in the hospital, and it looked like he would be for many more weeks. I sort of envied him the peace, but I thought, "I still hold him responsible for the condition of the contracts at this division."

General Dynamics phoned yesterday threatening to cancel that 1.7 million dollar contract for ground power units. Deliveries on the jet engine starters for the 106 fighters were a shambles. I couldn't think of a single contract right then that was on schedule and in the black!

"Why did we ever buy this factory anyway?" Our Concertone and American Avionics Divisions were making money, but I thought, "We may have bitten off more than we can chew here." I wondered if the people we bought it from had really made the profits here that they claimed. It had sure looked like a bargain to us then, but not today.

"If the supervisor hadn't gotten sick, I never would have been forced to dig into the details here so quickly myself. It seemed like every rock I turned over had a snake under it! Two hundred thousand square feet of snakes—what a mess! If this thing stays in a nose-dive and generates a lot of red ink, it could get pretty tense," I mused.

Then I thought about our underwriter on the recent stock issue. What a spot to put them in during the very first year! Then, "What about the bank? Our bank loan stands at $2,400,-000 and I wonder if they'll have the nerve to see us through if this thing goes sour? They weren't too keen in the first place on our acquisition. It wouldn't be unreasonable for some of the new stockholders to get a little 'exercised' if the stock started to skid! Who would believe we really didn't know these things back at the time of the stock issue? It would be hard for them to swallow that we had trusted others' word about the condition of the contracts.

"Boy, I see storm clouds coming—and fast! I'd better call Peter and give him the rest of the bad news I've just discovered. Pete's not going to like it, but he has to be told."

All these thoughts were ricocheting in my head when this command intruded: "Reread the Bible!"

"Reread the Bible?" My phone had been quiet for some minutes and this was unusual, so I sat there quietly for another moment before returning to the cost analysis on my desk. Then the thought came back: "Read your Bible—*again!*"

Something seemed to be coming. Could this be an answer to my prayer? "The only safe place to sort out the confusion about the Holy Spirit is *your Bible.*" But, I thought, "I already know what it said about the Pentecostal experience from all the teaching we've been getting over the past few years."

"Read it—again!" But why?

He was saying, "See what it *really* says." It seemed as though the Lord was saying, "You can't always depend on men—even *good* men. *I* will speak to you from My Word. Reread everything I have recorded about this. If you will read and reread the Scriptures I will wash your mind with the Water of My Word. Then you will know that My Word means just what it says. The meaning of My Word has at times inadvertently been manipulated. Certain men have bent My Word to match their lack of experience in the realm of My Spirit. They have made doctrines from their own interpretations."

John says (1 John 2:27), *But the anointing which ye have received of Him abideth in you, and ye need not that any man teach you: but as the same anointing teacheth you of all things, and is truth, and is no lie, and even as it hath taught you, ye shall abide in him.* And He went on in my thoughts, "You may also need the counsel of godly men on this search."

I prayed softly at my desk: "Who can I talk to about the Baptism with the Holy Spirit? Where can I find someone to help me?"

The answer came to my mind something like this: "Where would you go to learn about the gift of eternal life? Would you go to an atheist? Would you go to one who had never experienced salvation? If you are an earnest seeker concerning the work of Jesus Christ as Baptizer with the Holy Spirit, then ask one who has already met Him as their own Baptizer. Don't go to those in your present church since they have shared generously with you right up to the very limit of their experience with My Spirit."

That seemed reasonable. If I needed a new electronic circuit designed, I wouldn't go to my sheetmetal man, would I?

Over the next few days I got to reminiscing about my Christian friends. They had become such a delight and a comfort to me. What would they think if they knew I was looking into this Holy Spirit business? What if they found out about Virginia? What if I ever got into it myself? What would the pastor and my CBMC friends do? These were disturbing questions!

I coveted their respect and friendship with all my heart. I

had earlier lost most of my worldly friends when I became a Christian, and now I hoped lightning wasn't going to strike again! Well, the Bible says that fear of God is the Beginning of wisdom. Wisdom—I could sure use some wisdom. If I went through with this Holy Spirit business could I stand the frowns of my wonderful new evangelical friends? But if this be of God I must fear and trust Him above people.

My life seemed to be an endless row of decisions and choices, clear off and over the horizon—many of them big choices—ones that would make or break financially, reputation- and career-wise—now, spiritually. Right then it was clear to me that I would have to go on with God even if I lost the love of every other human on earth. "I'll have to choose God if I find this experience is real, even if everybody thinks I've gone off my rocker!"

Boy, this was tough! My spiritual and moral life was a jagged graph of ups and downs. Mostly downs! I sure didn't have much power, and if there was one thing that I knew, it was that George Otis needed more power from somewhere to live really for Christ. Suddenly, I wanted all that God had for me, enough to buck the whole world for it, if necessary. I was going to do it! I was going to look into this with the same passion that I focused on new projects in our lab. I would examine this under the best spiritual microscope—the Bible.

A three-week mixture of business pressures every day and intense hours at night in my *Scofield Reference Bible*—three weeks of research punctuated with visits to noisy churches that I'd never been inside before—and then it began to come.

It was that Word—it was almost jumping out of that *Scofield* now, and I respected the Bible as my Creator's operating handbook for me. "Yes, I see it, Lord, in 1 Corinthians 3:8: . . . *tongues* . . . *shall cease* . . . *knowledge* . . . *shall vanish away*. . . . And then in verse 10: *when that which is perfect has come* . . . *That which is perfect?* Why, that's *Jesus*, isn't it? And He isn't back yet." Of course—and knowledge hasn't ceased yet either! We sure won't need knowledge or faith or tongues either when we are with Jesus face-to-face, will we? Maybe these gifts haven't ceased after all!

"Yes, I see that, too, Lord. I really do have the Holy Spirit already, just as they say at my church. But so did those followers of Christ that He breathed on. It says, *He breathed on them* (John 20:22) and they received the Holy Ghost and that was before Pentecost. Now here are these *same* men standing with Him as Christ gave His last instruction. These very same men were also commanded by Jesus (Acts 1) to tarry in Jerusalem until they were endued with power from on high. Yes, they received the Holy Spirit but He said they also needed to be *baptized* with the Holy Spirit. They had the Holy Spirit, just as I have now, but Christ knew they needed the Holy Spirit in this other way, too. Just like me!

"And look at this! Those Ephesians were sort of like me. Those evangelists had been working in Ephesus and some of those Ephesians were saved. They made Christ Lord of their lives, and it says here they followed Christ's example and were baptized in water. Then the Apostle Paul is led to go through Ephesus where he asks *certain* disciples, *Have ye received the Holy Ghost since ye believed?* (Acts 19:2). They had already received from Christ the gift of eternal life; yet it was vital that they now meet Jesus again as Baptizer with the Holy Ghost! Just like me.

"Why, there is something else after all!" An excitement began to fill me! On and on those Scriptures went. The first time or two that I would reread a passage it would seem in my mind to mean the same as I had always been told that it should be interpreted. But continued rereading in obedience to the thought given to me in my Astro-Science office finally helped my understanding. Slowly these Scriptures began to say to my heart that which God had intended them to mean. It was a surprise to find that they simply meant *exactly* what they said! It is hard to *unlearn* a tradition. No wonder it's easier for people who haven't been weighted down with the traditions of men to receive the Baptism with the Holy Spirit.

Since then I have observed this strange spiritual phenomenon many times. Church A will teach that miracles and healings ended back in the first century after they had served their purpose to launch Christianity and after the Bible finally became available. This teaching and doctrine seem to be confirmed among the people in the congregation of church A. Sure enough, there are no miracles and no healings among these folks — just as the pastor teaches.

But two blocks down the street at church B things are somewhat different! The pastor of church B emphasizes that God is the same yesterday, today, and forever — that His name is still *Jehovah Rapha*, "the God that heals." Church B teaches that God is still dispensing His miracles and healing — and the people are expectant! On Wednesday night, one after another stand to tell of a deaf ear opened or a burn that left no scar — perhaps a miracle of finances as one had cried out to God for help.

The same Bible is used at both churches. Those same verses seemed to say one thing at church A and something different to the people of church B. God is so patient with His children. Both churches love God and love His Word, but it is vital that we not settle for less than God's best. He is still confirming His Word today by His mighty deeds among men.

Finally I was ready to pray enthusiastically and without reservations for the baptism. I was even ready to pay the price.

By now I had heard a number of testimonies of different people who had received — one in his car while he was driving down the highway and another in his shower one morning! Many received when they were alone somewhere praying. One young man said he was baptized with the Holy Spirit while he was out in the woods praying — and alone with God.

"That's for me," I thought. "That's the way I want it! I am a dignified executive. After all, I am a Presbyterian and we do things decently and in order." I didn't mind receiving tongues, for I had already heard Virginia's new prayer language and it was beautiful! Some others sounded pretty funny to me though, and so I preferred to receive this alone. I wasn't keen about making strange sounds in front of people that I didn't even know. "It will be better," I rationalized. "This way no one else's emotions will have an effect on me. I want to be very sure that this whole thing is of God and not the flesh." Now I was ready to pray.

"Dear Jesus, I know from my Bible that You are the Baptizer with the Holy Spirit. Please baptize me right now with the Holy Ghost. I want to be endued with Your power from on high. I can see in the Bible that the pattern evidence when they were baptized with the Holy Spirit was that they all spoke with new tongues. So please fill me with your Spirit, dear Lord, and give me a new language just like at Pentecost so that I, too, may know you have answered my prayer. Amen."

There, I had done it! I was all alone and waiting for Him to fill me with His Spirit. My door was closed and not a soul was around. He could give me this right now, and I would receive it quietly — decently and in order. Nothing happened! I struggled to surrender more. I finally said out loud, "Lord, I surrender!" But still nothing.

Days went by. The same prayer with different words and sometimes twice or three times a day. What was wrong? Here I was sacrificing everything, wasn't I? I tried surrendering still more — Standing up, lying on my back in bed, down on the floor. I prayed on my knees and then on my face! I prayed in the shower and in the car — even in secret at my plant. I was eager, but I still didn't realize that I was setting limitations on God as to just how and where He could meet me as Baptizer.

Jesus had paid His awful price for me — without reservations! But now I wanted His baptism *with* reservations. Panic! I began to search my heart and examine myself. "Was there still some unconfessed sin that was blocking me?"

Back to the Bible. Yes, there it was: Acts 2:4 *And they were all filled with the Holy Ghost and began to speak with other tongues, as the Spirit gave them utterance.* Something must be wrong with me. I thought, "Maybe I'm not worthy enough yet." Then I remembered that no one is ever "worthy enough." This doesn't depend on my worthiness but on Christ. There was no way I could justify receiving this from God. It is a gift and it is given to help us to become more like Him. About then I also remembered that I hadn't been worthy of His gift of eternal life either. But He had given it to me just the same.

Days later on a hazy Saturday morning, I was rolling down the San Bernardino freeway toward the El Monte plant. It was 9:30 in the morning and the traffic was light. I flipped on the radio and dialed across to 1390, KGER. (I wanted to listen to some Christian music.)

"Lots of work ahead of me this morning at the plant," I mused. Then a man with a clipped, eastern accent was telling about the Lunar Excursion Module development project at General Electric. Interesting! This was our field — aerospace hardware. "What kind of a radio program is this anyway? Why, this man is a Christian and he is saying right over the radio that he prays every day in English and in tongues before he starts work." In *tongues!* "His name is Doctor Rodney Johnson and he lives in Pennsylvania."

I rolled into the Astro-Systems parking lot and let the motor run. I wanted to find out where this program was coming from. They said it was from Clifton's Cafeteria, and that they meet every Saturday morning. Pulling out my pen, I wrote it down. "I wonder where Clifton's is? If I can possibly make it, I'll go next Saturday; maybe I can learn something — if I haven't received by then."

One week later I was carrying my breakfast tray up the stairs and over to a small table along the back wall. I moved the chair so I could watch the people coming in. "Surely," I thought, "there will be someone I know come here this morning." In they streamed by the dozens, several hundred of them, yet not a face I had ever seen before.

The program had been underway for a while, and it got a

little noisy! I squirmed, and suddenly the man at the microphone, Demos Shakarian, pointed his finger across the room
at me, "You there, please come up here a minute."

I thought, "He doesn't know me," and looked around to
see if there was someone else he meant. There wasn't, and I
started to weave through the people toward the head table.

He asked, "What's your name? Where do you work? What
church do you attend? Are you saved, Brother?"

Standing there before the microphone, I tried to answer his
questions, "Yes, I am saved. I received Christ a few years ago
at our church in Westwood."

Mr. Shakarian said, "Thank you, Brother Otis." It was obvious that my introduction was over and I started back toward
my table—when an idea came!

I whirled around and said into the microphone, "Say, I'd
like to take advantage of meeting all of you Christians here
this morning. For the last several weeks I've been praying
about something, and I would like to make a prayer request.
If you think about it this next week during your own prayer
time, would you remember me, please? I've been studying
my Bible and praying every day that Jesus would baptize me
with the Holy Spirit."

There was a pause about the length of an extra-fast lightning
bolt. Then eight hands were planted all over my head and
shoulders! It was the moment of truth!

There I stood, a Presbyterian businessman—a pride-choked,
stuffed shirt, determined to receive the Baptism of the Holy
Spirit in his own way. Alone and in secret. And suddenly that
stagnant tradition-choked well way deep inside of me just
burst into a gusher. Out of my mouth came a flow of words I
had never spoken in my life before—and without prompting
from a living soul! My hands floated upward in worship, and
I seemed lost with Jesus for twenty seconds straight. The
encounter with Christ was electrifying!

A half-hour later I learned the full humor of God's moment
of truth for me! Not only had I received the baptism before

three or four hundred people, but I had been called to the microphone during the segment of the program that was being broadcast over the radio!

On the way home, it became clearer to me. I hadn't really been as surrendered as I thought. I had been willing to surrender that most unruly member (my tongue) only in secret. I hadn't really trusted my utterly trustworthy God to meet me in any place and fashion that He should choose. He always knows what is the best and has a custom of understanding each of His children. Why, He even knows the number of hairs on my head! At last, unconditional surrender at Clifton's Cafeteria and finally, God had been able to drop the other shoe. And it had seemed as though every atom of my being was being recharged with the batteries of Heaven!

When I drove into the Bel Air carport that Saturday noon, Virginia was standing there watching. As I got out of the car she looked in my face. "It's happened, hasn't it?"

I smiled and said, "Now I don't feel left out any more."

8

Trouble Is a Servant

David said it first! *The plowers plowed upon my back: they made long their furrows* (Psalm 129:3). Paul of Tarsus knew it!

> *... in stripes above measure, in prisons more frequent, in deaths oft. Of the Jews five times I received forty stripes, save one. Thrice was I beaten with rods, once was I stoned, thrice I suffered shipwreck, a night and a day I have been in the deep. In journeyings often, in perils of waters, in perils of robbers, in perils by my own countrymen, in perils by the heathen, in perils in the city, in perils in the wilderness, in perils of the sea, in perils among false brethren. In weariness and painfulness, in watchings often, in hunger and thirst, in fastings often, in cold and nakedness* (2 Corinthians 11:23–27).

Paul continued to set these things into the perspective of eternity. He told of their great value in his life, in his ministry, and their role of preparation for eternity. Life isn't always a bowl of cherries for even the most mature and victorious Christian alive. Paul's troubles weren't some indication that he was out of God's will or walking in some great secret sin. The Christian life is a great University of the Spirit preparing us for eternity while still in this crucible of time. Many times we flunk certain tests and have to take them over and over and then over again until we finally pass.

Wise old Doctor Follette spoke in our home just a month before he saw Jesus face to face. He was one whose spiritual strength touched all, yet even his life had felt the sting of misunderstanding from some of his closest Christian friends.

His eyes were deep and radiant. You felt he could see into the depths of your soul — a man wonderfully filed, shaped, and blasted into the image of Christ by diverse trials as he pressed on toward that mark of the high calling.

Dr. Follette said it, too, "Don't fight it, don't run from it, don't be afraid when it knocks at *your* door. Let it come in. Receive it. Trouble is permitted by a loving Father who wants to bring something good out in you — for His own glory. He will never send it but to beautify you and to mold you more into the image of His lovely Son. He will not send you more than you can bear; make trouble your servant."

The Lord says, "See those ugly bumps of pride and spiritual lethargy there on your soul? Here, let Me scrape them off with the tool of this kind of trouble! Yes, it may hurt, and it may take a while, but you will be pleased with the new cosmetics of your soul after I am finished. That's it, my child, steady now, We will start here. I never waste my trouble surgery! I always know how much you can bear, and I always see you as the finished product right from the start."

For whom the Lord loveth he chasteneth, and scourgeth every son whom he receiveth (Hebrews 12:6).

Now trouble was doing its unwelcome but vital work on my own soul right after the sharp furrow of the Dick Mock luncheon firing from Lear. It really tore up an ugly cancer of pride and self-confidence. It tore me up, *period!* Only a deep gouge could have devastated such a hardened person as I was in preparation for God's dropping His first shoe of salvation.

Then came those long jagged furrows back and forth from the Astro-Systems debacle. One million two hundred thousand dollars fell from the asset side of my personal statement

when that El Monte plant turned out to be a lemon! A nightmare? You bet it was — at the time! But with spiritual hindsight
I could now see that the $1,200,000 loss was really the best
buy of my life. It was the furrow that produced enough desperation of soul to allow God to drop His other shoe on the
restless-climbing boy. Every dollar lost and every stress had
been loving preparation to make me willing to research those
Scriptures concerning a step I then considered so drastic as
the Baptism with the Holy Spirit.

Then came the riptide of forces and troubling circumstances
preceding the book! God's plowmen are still at work. Trouble,
agony of soul and pocketbook woes were all permitted by Him,
as I struggled with the leading to "Write the book!"

Those plowmen had now been busy for years and the furrows were long and deep. They hurt, and sometimes two or
three were plowing at the same time there. Some people need
only a few little furrows in their whole life — but I was different. It was hard ground and rocky, and I was stiff-necked, arrogant and self-confident. "Much plowing and harrowing is
called for in this field!" says the loving and wise Lord of the
Harvest.

So at long last I had been saved and then baptized with the
Holy Spirit. Surely now, I thought, "I've got it made." But still
that following shadow of the old Adam-life seems always to be
just waiting to rise up if permitted. The baptism wasn't instant
Utopia or some magic pill. *It* provided the potential, not the
end product.

My own life really was different after the baptism. If salvation had ignited the booster stage of my own spiritual rocket,
then the Baptism with the Holy Ghost had ignited the inser-
tion stage rocket that kicked me into His orbit — and I haven't
landed yet! And now I know that I never, never shall!

But it wasn't some easy, instant job. The baptism was a spiritual new tool to help me to cope with the corrosiveness of life
on this earth. The Christian life is our opportunity to be remanufactured and spiritually modified for all that lies ahead

in a long and glorious eternity. Difficult lessons in this hostile place are designed to prepare us for The Place we are pressing toward.

No, there is no arriving and there's no place to stop in this life. I sure knew that I wasn't a whit better than any other Christians who hadn't received. Hundreds of thousands of these Christians were far more spiritually mature than I. But of this I could attest: the new George Otis really was better than that old one — not better than anyone else — just better for having met the Baptizer.

Only God knew my full inventory of deficiencies, but now He had handed me a lovely new tool — one He had forged in heaven! This practical gift of the Holy Spirit was designed to help me along my journey in a hostile place that's not my home.

The spiritual walk through time into eternity is like a car with *no brakes* climbing up a hill. As long as you are pressing upward you are all right; but there is no place to stop on this spiritual hill called life. The moment you try to *park* you start to slide back. You must continue to move upward!

So it is with our spiritual journey. Some want to stop moving with salvation. They feel they have arrived at their ultimate destination so they are going to park there for the rest of their lives.

Others will park on a glorious camp-meeting high! Others want to park on a so-called deeper-life doctrine, and some want to pull over here and park on a miracle — perhaps here on this great healing experience or how about over here on the Baptism of the Holy Spirit and speaking in tongues! But alas, there is no parking on any experience regardless of how glorious or how genuine.

But maybe we *can* park on the shoulder of this great denomination or this Bible teacher or pastor. Regardless of how great any high point or spiritual attainment is, there is just no place to stop. We must press on, or back we start to slide again. There is no full attaining in this life — no arriving. We are pilgrims and we are journeying. Time enough to park when we are with Him!

No, I had not arrived! I had just changed roads in the last few years after roaring for that first thirty-four years, charging along with the accelerator to the floor board.

I had been on the road to Hell, and I was in a hurry. Christ Himself had picked me up and tenderly put me on His new road—THE WAY. I hadn't arrived; still struggling; moving slowly; sometimes in jerks; but TOWARD HIM.

I just couldn't say what the Baptism with the Holy Spirit really meant to others. Only they know its consequences in their own lives, but as for me, along with it a hundred things had gone *click* inside my being after my second major encounter with Christ.

And finally, I could sense a bit of what Samuel had spoken of concerning Israel's new King, *And the Spirit of the Lord will come upon thee, and thou shalt prophesy with them, and shalt be turned into another man* (1 Samuel 10:6). I prayed to God that He should now be allowed by me to work His works in my dark life—that I might not ever try to park on this experience and allow my life to roll too far backwards ever again.

With the baptism, new forces began to move and stir in my being, freer at last with my praises to God. My former dutiful kind of love had been turned into a raging affection for Jesus! Now, I could speak this love with my understanding and with the Spirit also. My hands suddenly were unshackled from the traditions of men and now seemed to float upward more easily in the praises due my Creator.

Then, too, a new hunger for the Word broke loose inside me that helped spawn a new ministry called Bible Voice. The work ultimately sent a million Bible and Bible study recordings throughout the world. But Bible Voice really attracted me first to satisfy *my* own needs and the recorded Word flowed like a crystal stream through my own soul.

Then like a giant hammer blow struck from heaven there was a bursting of the deadly chains of drink and bondage from

those ghastly pills! Astounding, to me! Nobody else but me
can ever really comprehend the magnitude of this miracle of
liberation.

And peace — real peace — the kind of peace I had never ever
known. Then there was the wonderful new love for Virginia.
Suddenly a good marriage had been instantly made a *great*
one! It was as though the capacity to love both Jesus and my
wife had been divinely stretched. Well, it simply affected
every department of our life together.

Fifteen months later, I was standing in the basement of a
Philadelphia hotel at my first Christian Booksellers' Conven-
tion. Did you realize that there are four thousand families
who operate, at great personal sacrifice, Christian Book stores?
God has raised up these people to serve His children with
Christian literature, supplies, and recordings.

After my Clifton's Cafeteria experience as I shared earlier,
my appetite for the Bible had grown. Harald Bredesen had
started to work on getting the Bible onto tape. He is the human
father of what is now Bible Voice. From this exciting concept
of Harald's I recorded a little of the Bible myself, and started
to carry a tape recorder with me in the car. It allowed me to
buy back otherwise wasted hours of driving between our
Culver City and El Monte plants. It had almost seemed like
God was riding with me and feeding my soul with His Word!

Faith grew in me, for it is a law of God's that *faith cometh
by hearing . . . the word of God* (Romans 10:17). All my life
I had fed the physical part of my being, three meals every
day. Now at last I was feeding the most important part — *my
spirit* — with the strengthening food of God's Word. The Bible
Voice ministry was then launched, and as I stood there behind
our little booth I knew that God had sent me to Philadelphia.
I had been clearly impressed to order this booth space months
before and now here I was with the tape recorders and our
new Bible tapes. My first impression of the CBA convention
was acres of books.

Dozens and then hundreds of Bible store owners began to file through the aisle in front of our booth, but none of them stopped! They seemed to make a little half-circle maneuver, shying away from this booth. Now we were displaying the very first Christian tapes ever offered to the booksellers and they just hadn't seen anything like them before. Our Bible Voice tape recorder must have looked out of place – like a little black bomb or something! We sensed this, but I still got more and more frustrated with every hour of their massive disinterest.

Dan Malachuk, a Christian friend, had come to help at the convention. We began to try different things. We would turn on the tape recorder and let the Bible blare out of the speakers; then we reorganized the booth. After that we painted a sign offering prizes for anyone who would stop to listen. In desperation, we finally tried going out into the aisle to invite people to listen to our taped Bible. Now it had been hours – and the first customer had yet to buy one of our new electronic Bibles.

Dragging up to my room at the dinner break, I was utterly discouraged. Opening the door I sank to my knees near the bed, and started crying out,

"Dear Lord, what's happening here? I thought Bible Voice was inspired by You, and that it was You who spoke to me months back to introduce Bible Voice here at the convention. But now I can't help but wonder whether this Bible recordings business is just something that was born out of my own mind? I need to know whether it is of me or of You. If You aren't in this work, I'm going to quit tonight, and I won't even stay for the rest of this convention without You. We've already spent twenty-five thousand dollars to bring this Bible recording effort this far, but I want to stop now if it's just a gimmick. I need to know whether You lead us to record the Bible on tape? Please tell me now somehow – I just can't face these booksellers anymore without knowing. Please help me, dear Father, in Jesus Name, I ask this!"

Within seconds a thought was impressed upon my mind! It
went like this: "Didn't I say that if need be I would make the
very stones to cry out!"

I said out loud, "Yes, Lord, I remember something like that.
It's somewhere in the Bible—that's a real encouragement to
me. I see it, the Bible speaking—You speaking on tape. Yes,
it could connect to Bible Voice. That's good. Thank you Lord."

Then the capper came! It was another thought and it was
like a question, "What is magnetic tape anyhow?"

I answered, "You know, Lord. Those Bible tapes are rib-
bons of plastic with iron oxide on the audio surface."

Then, the question, "What is iron oxide?"

I shot to my feet. I leaped there in the room trying to restrain
myself, "Glory! Glory! Glory! Oh, thank You, Lord, thank You.
What an answer! Oh, forgive me; for my unbelief. I'll never
again question its origin. You have shown me that Bible Voice
really was as an impulse from Your own heart.

"Iron oxide?" I had remembered that it is essentially
crushed and treated iron ore. *Rocks. Stones!* Literally, God
was now making the very stones to cry out His Word from our
Bible tapes. It was worth the whole Philadelphia trip in itself!

At the product display session immediately following this
prayer time those wonderful store owners began to stop and
listen to our tapes and our first two sales were made. Bible
Voice had been premiered!

Trouble Is a Servant

All of us know trouble—at least I hope we do;
   Trouble is a servant, but known as such to few.
We are taught to shun her and, if she comes too near,
   Seldom do we face her but run away in fear.
Good and bad must meet her, the universe around—
   Sinners, saints, kings and knaves—she comes where man is found.
Always make her serve you, for she can serve you well;
   Just HOW you may use her your life will always tell.

Trouble is but passive—it's by our power to will
  We make her either bless us or do the soul some ill.
How do you translate her from phrases filled with pain
  To messages of strength—from loss to endless gain?
By faith we see behind the outer frightful mask
  A servant in disguise, to do a gracious task.
Hearts may feel her wounding and life may suffer loss;
  Faith translates her working, as freeing gold from dross.
Trouble will discover to any yielded heart
  Hidden depths of power it only knew in part;
Sympathizing power, and love that understands;
  Strength to help another with trouble-tested hands.
Trouble will release you from self and make you kind,
  Adding new dimensions to heart and soul and mind.
Do not shun this servant, but look beyond her task
  To beauty she will work—for which you daily ask.
Always see in trouble a chance to grow in grace,
  Not a stroke of evil to hinder in your race.
Live the life triumphant above her fiery darts;
  Rich fruitage will be yours to share with needy hearts.

JOHN WRIGHT FOLLETTE

9

Fragrant Harbor

The big Cathay Pacific jet screeched, skidded, and yawed down that narrow runway in the sea. Peering through the Plexiglas window, the sky was blackish-blue. A galaxy of tiny lights were running up the hills. With a roar, the big turbines reversed it to a stop. Briefcase in hand, I stepped out the door onto the Kai Tak ramp. There's that smell again—like warm soggy straw. The smell of the Orient. Hong Kong (Fragrant Harbor) I'm back again!

It had been three-and-a-half years since God dropped the first shoe in that Presbyterian church. It seemed like a lifetime—or more. But it was just ten days since He had dropped the other one at Clifton's and here I was at the bottom of the world.

"Hello there, George, I'm over here," called the thin, spectacled importer I had come to see. Since I knew his own spiritual stand, I blurted out about that other shoe. He was ecstatic! Nothing stoic about this Chinese! Then we went on with the business I had come to discuss.

The next day in his Hong Kong office the phone rang. Long distance—from Bangkok. I shuffled through my papers until he hung up the receiver.

"Well, George, I'm glad you're here. God knew about your

timing. This is the night of our midweek service. That was the
pastor of our waterfront church and he's stuck in Bangkok. Tai
Airlines had engine trouble on the Hong Kong run and he
wants you to be our speaker tonight."

I gasped, "Oh, no, not me! I can't speak Chinese and I can't
preach. You take the service and I'll come over and listen to
you."

He said, "I can't—I'm already committed to speak at our
Kowloon church tonight so you'll just have to do it alone."

I pleaded, "But, I have never done it in my life. I can't speak,
what would I say?"

"You're just right for this. God knows what He is doing and
our people love to hear Christians from far away places. We
couldn't find anyone who lives much farther away! Maybe you
can give your testimony."

I saw he was serious and mumbled something. I was trapped,
and it was hard to keep my mind on the buying job for the rest
of the day. The obligation sort of hung over me from then on.
I prayed just about every hour on the hour, "Dear Lord, help
me. What can I say tonight?"

Walking out of the Peninsula Hotel that evening, I wasn't
sweating just from the heavy air—I was also sweating on the
inside, too. I walked past the line of rickshas on my way to the
dock. Then gliding past the darkened junks with their patched
sails, I sat on that Hong Kong ferry speeding up my prayers.
Just forty more minutes and I would have to stand up in that
church. Still no message and still no nerve!

Up to the fifth floor and into the room. There were maybe a
hundred Chinese milling around in little groups. Now they
were singing and the service is under way. The little pump
organ made a quaint sound and the singing was spirited. I
couldn't understand the language, but strained to hear the
Chinese equivalent of the words to "There Is Power in the
Blood."

Now I was a little frantic and slipped off my chair right on
the platform. I kneeled there in concern for the evening. "Dear

Lord, any minute now the interpreter will wave me to the podium. You must help me! What do You want to say to these people tonight?"

A series of vaguely connected thoughts came to my mind. If they could be put into words it would have gone something like this:

"Tell them for Me, that I long to be an intimate part of their lives. I'm not a doctrine—I am their loving and concerned Heavenly Father. I want to heal their sicknesses, solve their problems, take care of their financial needs, and resolve their marital crises. I want to be the Source of their every personal need. Not one need leave this room tonight carrying out a single problem that he brought in with him!"

Now the interpreter was motioning to me. I walked slowly to the speaker's stand and said, "I am a businessman and I didn't come to know Jesus Christ as my Saviour until I was middle-aged—just a few years ago. Most of you are far more mature in the things of the Lord than I, and you should be teaching me tonight instead. Just ten days ago I met Jesus Christ again in a brand new way for the second major encounter in my life with Him."

I told them briefly what had happened to me—how never before in my whole life had I ever had the courage to speak like this—and how before the baptism I never had the boldness to lead a single person to Christ in the several years since my salvation.

"You saw me kneeling up here just a few minutes ago. I was desperate before God and cried out to know His will and what I should share with you." And I started to tell them all that had come to my mind. "I suppose I might even say God asked me to tell you these things tonight. I believe that is really what happened as I prayed up here."

Scriptures were punctuating my story—verses from the Bible I had never memorized. Where were they coming from? They seemed to fit right in and support the things that I was telling them. It was exhilarating! I was feeling, for the first time, I suppose, an anointing to teach Christ. It was a very short message, and I returned to my seat.

Much talk in Chinese by my interpreter to the people. Two more hymns, with familiar melodies but the words were Chinese. Everybody got up at one time. I thought the service was dismissed and picked up my things. The people began to form lines and the interpreter was waving to me again.

"What do you want?" I asked him.

"We have just given them an invitation for personal prayer. We are going to pray for each person that has a need now — one by one."

"That's good. Go ahead; I'll wait here!" was my reply.

"But they are waiting for you to pray for them. It was through your mouth that God spoke tonight, and they want you to continue that ministry now. They are ready to receive from God, and it's time for you to start praying for them. There are many needs over in that line."

I was cornered again and we walked together over to the first person. It was an older Chinese lady who had been bothered that day with pains in the area of her stomach. As I prayed the interpreter would repeat in Cantonese. Sometimes there would be a big smile at the end of the prayer. Hands would shoot up from another at a certain point in my prayer and then excited chattering.

And here was a case, the interpreter said of a young woman with nervous tension and great fear. She had been like that for three years. Pointing my finger right into her face, "Why are you keeping that idol in your room? Jesus has given you the gift of eternal life and He won't stand for any other gods! Your fear is directly connected with your double-mindedness. Light and darkness can't live together without pain, confusion and defeat."

She burst into tears as this was interpreted, and fell to her knees nodding and crying out to God for forgiveness. It was true! How in the world did I ever happen to say that anyhow? It encouraged me, especially when the interpreter said, "She says the fear has left."

Later to another bent with chronic back trouble, I demanded, "Who is it that you hate so much? There is someone in your life that you have a terrible resentment for! Who is it? It's involved with your backaches. You must confess this and ask the Lord's forgiveness for allowing a root of bitterness to consume your spirit! Then go and make peace with whomever this is."

Again, the tears, and a head going up and down. "It is true," she said through the interpreter. "It is my mother-in-law who lives with us." She asked forgiveness and said she felt relief. On to the next one and then the next. . . .

Suddenly, there she stood.

Maybe thirteen, maybe eighteen. Who can tell among the Chinese? She wore the gray *shui-i* (pajamas) and stood with difficulty. Both hands had grown like little stiff claws. Her feet and ankles were distorted as a rag doll chewed by a puppy.

I never did find out whether she had been born that way or whether it came from some childhood disease. The skin grew between her fingers holding them in a rigid cluster. She was grotesque — except for her face.

Fear shot through me! Some of the needs we had been praying for were such that no one could tell for certain whether the prayers were immediately answered or not. But this one was different, oh, so different! I said to the interpreter, "What does she want?" (As if I didn't know!)

"She wants her body healed."

"Oh, Lord, this is too much for me." Now everyone was standing around watching. I shut my eyes and started to pray. I just couldn't look at her, but as I started, something came up in me. Hadn't God said He would take care of their needs? I started to pray for that girl as I had never prayed in all my life. I asked God to perform a miracle in her body. It was the longest prayer, I guess, that I had ever prayed. Perhaps a minute or more. I was spent!

I opened my eyes and looked at her. There she stood — exactly like she was before. There was nothing to do but move on to the next in line.

This troubled me, but there was work to be done and I couldn't stop now. It was clear God was moving for many others. Four or five minutes later I caught a glimpse of her out of the corner of my eye. There she stood in the same spot where we had left her — like a lonely, broken statue. I knew as if God had thundered from Heaven what was happening inside her mind. She was saying to herself, "This man said God told him that no one needed to leave here tonight until their needs are met by Him. I'm not going home until I have mine."

I shot across that floor and for the first time laid hands on that crippled teen-ager. Hard tears broke from my eyes and ran to my collar. I was half-angry and half-consumed with a kind of faith that I had never sensed. An unusual phenomenon happened during that prayer that had never happened to me. There came a sort of a fever in the palms of my hands.

I felt a burst of *unthrottled belief* and now I was shouting my prayers — half in love for the crippled child (and half-sounding like a command). I called out something like this:

"Satan you are finished! You get out of this girl's body! Loose her this instant! I show you the shed blood of Calvary."

And then, "Now, dear Jesus, lay your healing hand upon her. Speak that word to every cell of her body. Heal her now, Lord, from the top of her head to her feet. Please."

I opened my eyes — He had done it!

Her arms and hands were in the air and she started to walk in a circle crying softly, "Hallelujah! Hallelujah!" which sounds the same in every language I ever heard. The Bible says, *And he took him by the right hand, and lifted him up: and immediately his feet and ancle bones received strength.*

And he leaping up stood. . . . leaping, and praising God (Acts 3:7, 8).

I became very emotional for a few seconds. This Presbyterian was caught off guard and I must have sounded like David when the Ark of Covenant rolled back into Jerusalem!

And that night, the girl wasn't the only one healed—I was too! My Westwood church believed that miracles had ceased in that first century when the Bible was completed—that we are now in a dispensation that no longer needs the miraculous and the Gifts of the Spirit anymore. We had put away "childish things" but my Jesus had just shown me *His doctrine* in the body of the child. He had confirmed His Word in her flesh.

Ten days earlier my Lord had exploded something inside me, and this night was an outworking from that encounter. From the effect of God's dropping that other shoe, I had somehow been given a new capacity to believe. Before I had believed *with my head* that Jesus had done His mighty works of healing and miracles back in the first century, but now I had seen Him flash His mercy and power today. When Jesus re-created the broken body of that girl I knew that He really is the same yesterday, today, and forever—just as He says.

Riding back across the bay I praised God for this High Adventure! And I could hardly wait to tell Virginia as I hurried toward the overseas operator in the hotel lobby.

10

Satan's Showcase

Coming here was always like a kick in the stomach! Rain drove out of the four o'clock darkness as I lunged across the ramp toward the customs shed. The wet envelope of passport documents and travel checks was in one hand, and my Pan American flight bag was swinging from the other shoulder. On the slow drive into Bombay my tired body was jostled and my spirit depressed as we moved through the darkness of the outer suburbs.

It was like a festering scab on the face of the earth! A preview of the tribulation where peace is often sung while violence rages within her gates. It had been two weeks this time, moving and speaking from Agra to Trivandrum. I was leaving for home tomorrow.

Home! It sounded like heaven after this—maligned, despised, America, now the focus of wrath from the spirit of Antichrist. Perhaps it's the last country standing in his evil path. After this visit back to India, the criticism of America and the strident screams about poverty took on a new perspective.

Wonderful America! Her creed may best be expressed by one of her lovely states. The Hawaiians say, UA MAU KE EA O KA AINA I KA PONO—THE LIFE OF THE LAND IS PRESERVED IN RIGHTEOUSNESS!

My mind went back to the quick trip just concluding: the driven Madras and Benaras worshipers, the crooked temples covered with hundreds of bas-relief figures in unspeakable postures of sex perversions. I recalled thousands stepping across the stiff, ashen-faced man lying dead on the sidewalk from starvation. None of the throng broke stride as they rushed along to somewhere. So what? Hadn't they seen death in the open hundreds of other times? Weren't there 550 million more to take his place?

I recalled the mind-boggling paradox of the tons of beef walking around through those streets. They weave almost arrogantly through the taxi lanes and near the still form that had just given up his life crying out for food. Starvation stalks while the cattle walk free and unmolested throughout the great city.

The geometry and romance of Taj Mahal is blemished as you peer from her river porch to see the great prison there on the far bend of the river. It is the Red Fort from which the Taj's builder sadly viewed its beauty from his prison window — locked there by his own son. Everything here seemed flawed!

Standing at the crematorium in Bombay, we watched the stone platforms busily smoking their dreadful blue-white smoke. The sign reads, ONE RUPEE FOR USE OF THE CREMAT-ING BIERS — PLUS WOOD. Fourteen cents! Yes, it's cheap to die in India.

Business was good here. The stone platforms were never cold — three or four carrying this one — only two with this poor fellow. Eleven weeping friends bring another. He must have been rich. Rich for here, that is. They didn't come in caskets or on stretchers. They came slung over the shoulders of men — inert, lifeless, to be dropped rudely on a pile of wood. I couldn't watch anymore as they lit the stacks.

I shuffled out across the grassless, rock-strewn field. Suddenly I stopped! These weren't rocks. What were they? Oh, no! Bones and skulls, thousands of them. It was the refuse

field! They had to clean off those platforms didn't they? Was
I awake or asleep? I was awake all right—it was even more of
a nightmare with your eyes open!

A mile away the great birds were gracefully circling. God
was slowly unlocking a spiritual mystery for me on this trip.
Revelation! The great birds circled, and then broke rank as at
a shot. Down they came in disorganized panic. Every bird for
himself now! It was another terminal of a different religious
sect—a terminal, that is, where the bodies move on into an
oblivion. No cremation for this class. It was against their
highly disciplined religious system. Burning was blas-
phemous, and their gods forbid it. The corpse was swiftly
picked clean by the birds!

The refreshing segment of my visit had occurred earlier in
the week, and it had made the long trip here worth coming.
The acre-square of leaf coverings lay over dry stubble of the
drained rice paddy. The floor was mercifully protected from
the cloudless south India sky by a bamboo framework and
then laced with palm branches. Four thousand thin dark bodies covered the floor as they sat quietly—tightly woven together like a living carpet.

The Mar Thoma church was ancient in origin (to any place
other than Mother India). It was founded on one of the mis-
sionary journeys by bold Thomas who had walked with Jesus.
It was summer convention time in Kerala State. What a privilege to share with these wonderful followers of my Jesus as I
stood there on a dirt mound. It was an altar acceptable to the
Lord. But not even here were we free from the constant reminder of the powerful spirit princes of this land.

Halfway through my testimony came a rustle toward the
eastern side of our palm arbor cathedral—then cries of fear
and a great scattering of the carpet of people! The Old Ser-
pent had entered in the form of an adder to protest our intrusion into his own personal domain.

Now from my taxi it was growing light. The outline of cow-
dung huts along the bank emerged. These were the homes of

the prosperous. Earthly wealth is relative. The next class was sleeping along that road on cots, their little piles of bent and broken possessions underneath—their only home, never knowing a roof. Then came the poor, almost covering the rest of the area. Curled into tight balls, legs drawn up for warmth, they speckled the sidewalks and the stairways. A few had cloth to cover them. Others, with just the soiled clothes on their backs, were sleeping under a bush or a car. Then it came to me!

Satan had unwittingly spread a great display across the face of this subcontinent. It was a showcase of Satan—this blasted hulk of a nation of 550 million souls walking today, many to die tomorrow under the trampling feet of the living. They are exhausted and starved, flowing into eternity—ever blinded to God. Knowing only to serve deceiving gods in disciplined obedience, they march endlessly into a Christless hell.

Staggering! Mind blowing! Missionaries to India have long felt that same awful stab of helplessness. This trip was highlighting the ghastly drama of India writhing under the heel of the prince of the power of the air. How had he ever hidden this showcase of his wares from my people? —this awful display of the fruits from following his own false religions?

Now those spirit princes working under the direct control of Lucifer himself, were moving to invade our western world. Manifestations of their arrival are increasing: the flood of books proclaiming the secrets of spiritual life in the form of books on Hinduism, reincarnation, Krishna, Yoga, transcendental meditation. A new flood of Indian art objects and clothing and that heady incense of the East! They all gain easy entrance into the open mind and vulnerable drug-culture crowd across our mountains and plains. I remembered the thousands of hideous demon-possessed Indian "holy men"—the original hippies.

The guru and the swami were idolized and publicized by the Beatles and our Hollywood set. New shrines and religious centers appear. The glassy-eyed, cross-legged youngsters with the long hair sit transfixed on the grass, and the sound of the sitar becomes more common daily. They say, "Look to the East for enlightenment." You shall find it in India and Tibet, Kashmir, and Burma. The secrets of life and God! Joy and serenity and peace are there. The dark angels from the pit of hell are now flying low in the West!

I had seen the fruit of Satan's hand. I had seen poor India's tears, and I had seen terror in the open eyes of her dead—the prostrate man lying on the sidewalk in Satan's province. I have seen her dead being paraded to the burning piles, and I had heard the lie: "Don't touch that cow—it may be Christ or my father reincarnated!"

The beef walked free while the people on whom design had been lavished in the image of the Father, the Son, and the Holy Spirit lie broken everywhere! A colossal ecology nightmare! It's the home of Gandhi, but also of the black hole of Calcutta. Satan's showcase indeed! India is a heart-rending display of a people playing the grim game of follow-the-leader —walking the death march passively behind the father of lies: Satan himself.

Even now he is whispering his deadly enticements to my own people to the accompaniment of tinkling bells, incense, and the strange sound of the sitar. Oh, how I loved Jesus that Bombay dawn!

11

Heavenly Laughter

Then there was the time God worked out an unusual trip for us! Both Virginia and I listened on phone extensions as Chuck Woehrle called. (Chuck was a new Christian friend of ours who was working for 3M.) He was pouring out the story from his home in Minneapolis. "Dr. Fred Smith is dying of cancer! Fred's life has been so full of Jesus — no one knows how many students have been saved through his witness. He's the head of the Biochemistry Department here at the University of Minnesota.

"He is very close to Billy Graham and to the whole team," Chuck continued, "I somehow have the nerve to believe in God for a miracle for him here. All the specialists at the clinic agree that it's terminal. But Fred is still witnessing to the nurses and doctors — as if it's they that are in need instead. He is just fantastic! Katie, his wife, is holding up well and all of the prayer groups here are praying. I just wanted to ask you to pray for Fred in your home meeting out there."

I don't believe that I ever got a stronger spiritual signal from the Lord in my life. Both Virginia and I agreed, and in a couple of days we had our boys in the car headed for Minnesota. We played hymns, read the Bible and read a number of books on healing that we had bought before leaving. One of us would drive while the other read aloud, through state after state.

Faith soared with the miles and our expectancy grew that Dr. Smith would be healed. It seemed that everyone in Minneapolis knew about Dr. Smith's situation. What a spot, we thought, for God to prove to the skeptics that He is still in the same healing business just as He was when Jesus walked the shores of Galilee.

The trip was rewarded by our hours with this giant of a spirit! Fred knew the Lord could do it and believed with us for victory. We laid our hands on him in the Name of Jesus, and read those assuring Scriptures to him again and again. We came against the infirmity that was at work in his body. We cursed the awful cancer in his frame and commanded it to shrivel, in the Name of Jesus Christ.

One day at the hospital Fred said, "George and Virginia, since you've come all the way here from California, would you mind going down the hall to pray for a little friend who has terminal Lupus. It's a blood disease. Little Barb loves the Lord. Will you pray for her?"

We had time for Barb all right, but we were shattered when Fred died! His little friend was also sick unto death, but Barb felt the miracle surge of Jesus the Healer flow right through every cell of her body. She was instantly healed by the Lord! And when our prayer time for her healing was finished, we told her mother what the Bible says about Jesus as Baptizer with the Holy Spirit.

"Yes," the mother said, "we would like to have prayer for this fulness of the Spirit, also." The little girl quietly surrendered to Him and Jesus baptized her with the Holy Spirit. Barb had been endued with new Power from on high as an "extra bonus" along with her healing. We have since received cards from Barb at Christmas telling of her ongoing love for Christ and assuring us about her health.

Surely God's ways are above our understanding. It was hard for us to understand how wonderful Fred, the giant in the faith, was not raised up after our long trip there. And such a twist that the little girl we hadn't expected to meet should instead feel God's surge of new life! But I was given this Scripture concerning Fred Smith: *The righteous perisheth, and no man layeth it to heart: and merciful men are taken away, none considering that the righteous is taken away from the evil to come. He shall enter into peace: they shall rest in their beds, each one walking in his uprightness* (Isaiah 57:1, 2).

Then there was a painful day sometime back when the doorbell rang twice! It rang during an acute money-worry phase stemming from a financial misunderstanding. The last few dollars from our bank account had just gone into Bible Voice to honor two important bills. The check from our Oregon land project hadn't come through that month at all. A phone call to Land Investment Research revealed the reason: "It's time to pay the annual land taxes and there won't be any further checks for two more months."

Boy, this was pretty depressing! We had felt financial closeness from time to time, but this wasn't "closeness" this was it! We were *out of money!* Not *almost* this time, but *out! out!*

In the past, a quick run through the pockets in my clothes closet had been rewarding. Usually there would be a five-dollar bill or a few ones hiding in some suit. We raced again through every pocket expectantly. Thirty-five cents! Big deal!

The groceries were low, but not out. "We will make it somehow," I said. (I still had some stock to put up for sale.) "Maybe this will bring in something, but not for weeks yet—at best. What about now? What can we do this week for groceries and school lunches?"

Then the door bell rang. (It was the front one!) Virginia opened the door and there stood Chuck and Ila Perkins. Virginia was a bit surprised, and said, "It's so nice to see you. What are you two doing over here in the middle of the day?"

Chuck had been photographer for the Los Angeles *Times*, but he was out of work now. He had accepted Christ, and he had then been filled with the Spirit at our Sunnyslope house just a year ago. Chuck and Ila had many little mouths to feed, and I sure had to hand it to him. These days seemed to glow more with every new trial. He had really come along rapidly as a new believer. Virginia looked at his shoes. They had seen better days — and it was the only pair he owned, too. She wondered if my shoes would fit him.

After some sharing about what the Lord had been doing in their lives, Ila pulled out an envelope and put it in Virginia's hand, declaring, "The Lord said to bring this to you."

It was fifty dollars in cash! Virginia protested. "No, you mustn't do it. We just couldn't take this from you folks. Chuck doesn't even have a job yet!"

Then Virginia's head dropped in stunned silence as the tears welled up in her eyes. "Thank you, dear people, for your sensitivity to the Lord. We really are in a bind this week. The Lord surely knew and provided through you." It was humiliating — neither of us had really wanted anyone to know of our needs, and it was difficult for us. We had learned how to abound and now we were getting an important lesson on being abased!

Later that evening, after I got home from the office, the door bell rang again! This time — the back door. Virginia opened it and Harald and Gen Bredesen stood there with their arms laden down with boxes and packages!

Harald said commandingly, "Open that freezer door; we want to share with you from our abundance."

"Oh, no," I thought, "Not again so soon!" Then I insisted, "Harald, you just can't *do* this." All the time I was saying "You can't *do* this," Gen and Harald were piling frozen dinners, roasts, fish, and other items into our empty freezer. We were sort of numb as we all paraded into our living room. Still standing, Harald handed me a check — a big one!

He said, "Brother, this is the most fun I've had in a long time!"

I protested, "You people have already done too much for

us. You've brought encouragement to our spirits; you've helped put flesh on the bones of our own soul. But you just can't do *this!*"

Harald waved while he sort of pivoted around the room. "But we never had a chance to give you anything material before. You've always seemed unapproachable in this area— and now God has given us the privilege of blessing you in this way. This might be our only chance, so please, George, take it or you'll be robbing us of our own blessing."

As we sat down now, strength was flowing into our weak souls, and Harald began to laugh that infectious laugh of his and then we all joined in. It really was a hilarious scene! Here we sat in our great, old bargain-basement mansion. People would hardly imagine that its door bell would ever ring this way—twice!

With the sting of it gone, much laughter and thanksgiving bubbled out for our Christian friends and the mercy and provision of our generous God. He had shown us that He could provide for us in ways beyond calculating.

Consider the lilies of the field, how they grow; they toil not, neither do they spin: . . . even Solomon in all his glory was not arrayed like one of these (Matthew 6:28, 29). Painful, precious, needful lessons. Etching and filing ugly rough spots on our soul to make us a little more into the image of His flawless Son! Thank you, Lord.

One weekend while still in the middle of this manuscript I flew back to Michigan where Joe Ninowsky, a Detroit businessman friend, had scheduled a series of meetings. The first was a Friday night home meeting in Grosse Pointe where about thirty couples gathered at the handsome estate of a prominent Detroit attorney. All but a few that night were Baptists and they had asked me to share with them about the work of the Holy Spirit today.

When the formal part of our meeting was over, sixteen filed upstairs for further instruction about the Holy Spirit and for prayer. Just as we began, a lady opened the door and asked for our help. "I have been in considerable pain tonight. Could you pray for me before you start?"

We pulled out a chair for her. Then I was impressed to ask these Baptists who had gathered in the room to lay their hands on her and pray instead of my doing it. It is probable that none of them had ever before "laid hands" on anyone for healing prayer. Slowly and awkwardly they walked over and several timid prayers for healing were spoken out. Then the lady testified of relief and left apologizing for the interruption.

Three or four minutes later one of the Baptist businessmen sitting on the bed spoke out, right in the middle of my instructions. Very haltingly he told how he had never before given a testimony, but now sensed a strong urge to tell everyone what had just happened.

He rapidly turned his head back and forth. Many of them knew about his infirmity. For years he had been unable to turn his head at all and told us how it had been sort of locked. Then he took deep breaths of air and blurted out that he hadn't been able to do this for five years! God had healed him right when he had placed his hand on the sick lady and prayed for her. None of us had prayed for his healing that night, but the Lord honored his own obedience as he had ministered in prayer for another's infirmity.

His whole testimony was moving and the room was suddenly filled with faith! All but one fully met Jesus as his Baptizer during the next twenty minutes.

A law of God was at work in both of those healings. The Lord honors obedience and blesses the Christian who is ministering, as well as the one being ministered to. *Give, and it shall be given unto you* (Luke 6:38) applies to our ministering as well as our money. Satan is always whispering, "Wait a little while. You aren't quite ready yet to move out in ministry. Study some more first." Well—he's a liar! Most Christians have more spiritual knowledge than they ever use.

The Lord wants us to start using what spiritual knowledge

we do have, and then He will bless us with more. Seize every opportunity to share Christ and pray for those in need. As you are led by His Spirit you will find Him backing your obedience. It is vital to study to gain more knowledge but equally important that we use that spiritual knowledge we have.

Some months after becoming a Christian there developed in me a new conviction about business entertainment. For years I had taken for granted that it was essential procedure in business to wine and dine your customers. This is a deeply entrenched business practice.

After becoming a Christian this began to trouble me! It clashed with the Word of God and I began slowly to phase it out of my business while at the same time worrying that it was a great sacrifice. I felt sure that it would cost me thousands and that we were losing our sales competitiveness.

Then one day I spilled my problem out to a close customer friend who had been a recipient of our largesse.

"George, let me put your mind at ease," he declared. "Many buyers will accept those boozing and partying nights on the town, but in the cold light of dawn we feel safer placing our business with you fellows who don't carouse and, on whom we can better depend. Sometimes we glibly thank a fellow for partying us, but later resent that he has led us to play the fool! We don't like to lose our own self-respect this way, either, you know."

It was a great practical sermon! I have since observed that our own sales results have actually *improved* since abandoning this practice. Going with God is never a sacrifice. It was a surprising and a delightful discovery.

12

Christ Rattles the Gates

"Good morning, Mr. Otis," said an unfamiliar voice over my office phone. "This is John Hinkle. Would it be possible for you to have lunch with me today? If you're free I'll drive out to your office and pick you up around noon." It was during one of those stretches when the days and weeks were running far short of my needs.

The curtain of this present age is falling and clues that this is that last generation seem to be dropping everywhere; the morning newspaper, along Sunset Strip, the voice of the newscaster, rockets on the Golan Heights, and stories in *Time Magazine* confirm this colossal fact.

It hangs in the air; all nature groans — the true church is poised and breathless! This awareness of His soon return had moved me in recent months to say *yes* to every spiritual opportunity. We were just in the process of redoubling our efforts to speed up our flow of our Bible recordings. When Hinkle's call came, I was preparing to leave for a board meeting at the Infonics plant in Santa Monica, and had just finished the last rewrite of our *Crisis — America* book. (This was the message Harald, Pat Boone, and I had given alerting Christians in America to watch God's timepiece and awaken to the spirit of Antichrist within our gates. It's an urgent call to prayer for our nation — exhortation for the Christians to *occupy* until Christ comes.)

So Hinkle's call had caught me when I was a little tired and feeling pressed. Over the past few weeks I had been saying to myself "I must get more selective about my schedule. I can't respond to everything, and I must begin to cut down on all but the most potential." Almost wearily, I replied, "No, Mr. Hinkle, I can't do it today. Why, did you want to see me and what is your work?"

"My name is Reverend John Hinkle. Yesterday a friend gave me a copy of Pat Boone's book *A New Song*. Are you the George Otis mentioned in it? You are? Good. Well, I thought I would read a few pages in bed last night before turning out the lights. About twenty minutes later I sat straight up and couldn't stop until I had finished the last page at 3:30 this morning! I've never been so moved. I wasn't able to put it down. Mr. Otis, I want to know more about this and hoped you might be able to tell me. I am the pastor of the Unity church near Wilshire and Western in Los Angeles."

"Now," I thought, "this is the very sort of thing that I have to weed out of my life. My time belongs to the Lord and I can't do everything. I must learn to say no to some of these things that have little or no potential for Christ." I had a vague impression of Unity as being a sterile old denomination — something like a big religious club. My own idea of the thinking of some of their ministers went like this: Love and positive thinking are the big things! The Bible is a wonderful literary treasure, but not necessarily all really God's Word, of course. Jesus was a great Teacher and remarkable Prophet — but not necessarily virgin-born of God. Very good people — strong on social works with a little reincarnation woven in here and there.

So I replied, "Thanks for the invitation, Reverend Hinkle, but maybe another time; I have just finished the rewrite of a book this week and there's a frightening stack of work that has built up on my desk."

But he was persistent, "Would you mind taking a look at your calendar to see *when you can* spare an hour with me? I don't mind waiting, and I would like to take the first luncheon opening you have — if it's all right with you."

He was being a pest, and I didn't know how to get out of it. Fortunately, I could tell him that it was nine days before I had a clean page. But he said, "I'll take it. Would you mind marking it down? I'll be at your office about twelve o'clock."

At 11:50 nine days later, Reverend Hinkle was sitting in my outer office. We got in the car and steered toward the Farmhouse restaurant. I had secretly hoped the nine days would have cooled his curiosity, and that I would then be able to use this time more profitably. But here he was!

A bright and pleasant man — very easy to be with. I somehow started to share with him about a remarkable event I had experienced at a Christian mountain camp the previous Saturday. Rev. Dan Kricorian's mens' retreat had developed steam as my day of ministering unfolded. . . . *the word of God is quick, and powerful, and sharper than any twoedged sword* . . . (Hebrews 4:12). The Bible is supernatural and the one commodity that will survive earth itself.

It is written, . . . *and he cast out the spirits with his word and healed all that were sick* . . . (Matthew 8:16). And so it had gone as God's theme developed at the mountain retreat. The teaching was interrupted from time to time as one of the men would move to the center of the room for prayer. The Spirit of God was melting these businessmen's hearts as the Word just seemed to pierce their souls! And they were being peeled of their reluctance to receive personal prayer. One and then another began to move to the prayer chair, and a number received a real touch from God. More started to come. Some spilled out sordid stories of marital iniquity or impossibly knotted personal situations. Prayer would follow from the other men.

Then another would cry out for God's help for a financial crisis Then two were moved to sit in proxy for a son on dope and a runaway daughter. Then still another prayer for a chronically painful prostate condition—and so it had gone through the day, with God wonderfully moving for His sons. He was dispensing His blessings and there was deep joy. Grown men wiped tears from their faces.

Chuck De Frenzo was a fireman who shared his own burden. Something sinister was happening to the hearing mechanism inside each ear. Portions of the hearing apparatus were slowly receding—just shriveling up! The specialists told him there was no cure for this type of disease, and that he would be deaf in both ears. Chuck had gotten permission to retune the siren on his rig, so that the frequency of its scream wouldn't pain his troubled ears quite so much.

It happened during the final evening's session. I was concluding by simply reading aloud a chain of Scriptures that God had given me. Sixty men sat in a horseshoe shape around the high-ceilinged room. They were facing me as the big blaze in the fireplace crackled at my back. We were reading from Job 26:11–14.

> The pillars of heaven tremble and are astonished at his reproof. He divideth the sea with his power, and by his understanding he smiteth through the proud. By his spirit he hath garnished the heavens; his hand hath formed the crooked serpent. Lo, these are part of his ways: but how little a portion is heard of him . . . ?

It was right here that *it happened! But the thunder of his power, who can understand?* (v. 14).

Chuck shot to his feet, interrupting and holding both hands to his head, "I can *hear!* I can *hear!* God has healed my ears!" And He really had.

It was three days before we heard the final chapter of Chuck's story. I had spoken at Kingman Hall in Claremont the previous night and Chuck was there again. He asked me if he could tell the people about his healing. He repeated this story, but continued to tell of the unusual ending.

Chuck had gone down the mountain from the men's retreat that night and told his wife about his miracle. Then he went to sit in his usual chair to read before going to bed when he remembered his glasses. Three weeks before Chuck had given in to the demands of his weakening eyes when he had found himself holding his reading material farther and still farther from him. He ran out of arm and had finally broken down and gone to an oculist. The new reading glasses had been a blessing and so he called, "Honey, would you please hand me my reading glasses."

He started to read again, but there was something wrong. Chuck looked again and the print was blurred and he wiped the lenses. Then he slipped off the glasses, looking at the page without them.

"Good night!" God had thrown in a bonus up on the mountain as Job 26 had thundered into his ears! The Lord had healed his eyes and Chuck's new forty-five dollar glasses were junk—just an expensive reminder of a miracle!

His Lord was the same as in the Book of Acts and right here in the twentieth century! I caught myself, "Why was I telling Reverend Hinkle these things?" But John sat there, nodding his head and making just the right sounds. He seemed to pull it right out of me as he sat like a baby bird with its mouth open for more food.

We were back at my office now, and as I slipped out of the car, he said, "I know how busy you are, Mr. Otis, but would you mind looking at your calendar pad again? Before I go would you see if you can find another hour for me later? You haven't told me about the Baptism with the Holy Spirit yet."

With the words, "I know how busy you are, Mr. Otis," my heart broke and I saw a despicable picture of myself! God showed me the blackness of my sin in that flash. In the activity of these end-time days, our spirit can grow numb and calloused from "works." The gentle and sensitive spirit of the Dove can flee if we succumb to the dulling beat of Christian activity. "To the work! To the work!" can sometimes stupefy the spirit. Subtly, the work became more of *self* than of Christ. No wonder that Jesus would leave the throngs clamoring for His ministry at times. He would draw aside for a little season to be alone with the Father.

In that instant, I was shown how I had judged this man and his people to be unworthy of *my* precious time. I had written him off as beyond hope, and I had tendered my judgment as though I had the right. It was an ugly picture — and it was all me!

"John, please park and come on in; we'll talk about it right now." Then, "Evelyn, please hold my calls until I buzz you," I said as we walked by her desk into my office. When I closed the door, it was 1:25. I said, "John, do you remember a specific moment in your life when you asked Jesus Christ to come in and become the Lord of your life forever?"

"If you are asking whether I am a Christian, I have always loved and taught Jesus and His love for all mankind," replied Reverend Hinkle. "I have been serving my people in Christ Church Unity and expressing this truth to the best of my ability. But I have grown restless in the last two years. I have finally sensed there is something missing. I hoped that something new might be added to my life. I thought maybe it's this power of the Holy Spirit, and that's why Pat Boone's book raised such a fire in me!"

"That's wonderful," I said, "but John, you haven't answered my question completely yet." Then I went ahead to review how it isn't possible to meet Jesus Christ in His office as Baptizer with the Holy Spirit until first we are absolutely sure that we have met and accepted Jesus Christ in His prime office as Redeemer. We reviewed Christ's words about the religious Pharisees of His day and reviewed the history of fallen man from Eden onward — how our loving Father had devised this one and only Way to retrieve His disobedient children. We went over God's formula and the necessity of precisely following His salvation provision through His Son, Jesus Christ.

John wanted to be absolutely sure that he had first taken

full advantage of Christ's office labeled SAVIOUR before he knocked on that office door marked BAPTIZER.

Right then down on his knees, John asked Jesus to come into his heart and invited Him to assert Lordship over his life. He had made absolutely sure and now was up off his knees. As he rose, John said, "George, now can we pray for the baptism?"

"No, John—I feel that we're still not quite ready yet—in a minute maybe." Then together we started to review how men have always tried to sneak around God and get information or assistance from some other source. How Jesus had said, *I am the way, the truth, and the life: no man cometh unto the Father, but by me* (John 14:6). We recalled that the Tower of Babel had been built by men trying to reach God through their own human system and how God wouldn't have any part of it—not then or now!

We talked of how people seem always to be trying to yank aside the curtain of time, and sneak a look into the future. God tells us that He is the only Omega; that only He is the end and that we are to give no thought for the morrow. The future belongs to the Lord! *Today* is what men have to work with. Man's frantically increasing efforts to break down the laws of time and steal a look into the future are making the spiritualists and the astrologers rich. It seems that man just won't trust tomorrow to God.

The astrologers, the soothsayers, the wizards that peep and mutter, the necromancers, the magicians—they are still with us today! The new Satanic Church, the seances, the crystal-ball gazers, the tea leaves, the cards, the Ouija board, ESP, reincarnation, the Oriental religions, transcendental meditation (Deuteronomy 18:9-12), and the whole foul occult— how God hates these things!

Reverend Hinkle and I recalled how King Saul had slipped out of camp one night, unwatched, on his way to the witch of Endor. Saul couldn't wait either—he was determined to get a look into the future!

That big Philistine army was camped out there, and he just

couldn't wait to find out how the battle would go tomorrow. He couldn't trust tomorrow to God either. Saul found out all right, but he paid the inevitable price for seeking information about the future through another source—the source God so abhors! from the forbidden spirit world of the demon and the fallen angels—from Satan's realm. Did you realize that any source other than from God and His Word is so deadly dangerous?

Satan has a limited amount of information all right, but it's costly! The words lashed against Saul's ears. They said in essence, "For this, Saul, I will require your very life on the morrow." And the next day, saw the huge king pierced dead by the sword and hanging naked by his feet as a grizzly trophy before the taunting stares of his enemy! The Bible says, *The secret things belong unto the Lord our God: but those things which are revealed belong unto us and to our children for ever, that we may do all the words of this law* (Deuteronomy 29:29).

John Hinkle asked cleansing and forgiveness in Jesus' name for anything during his whole life that he may have done in spiritual ignorance. He didn't want to hinder the coming of the Holy Spirit. John was washed with the Blood of the Lamb and made whiter than snow, sealing off by this repentant prayer any possible doors from his past still open to the forces of darkness. We had earlier talked about how essential it is to block off any possible opening to the unholy spirits of this world before seeking God's Baptism with the Holy Spirit.

John's head was up again and I anticipated his words this time. "Now George, are we ready? Can we pray now for the Baptism with the Holy Spirit?"

I smiled. "Yes, John, praise God, it's time."

Reverend John Hinkle, pastor of that huge Unity Church near the Miracle Mile, asked his Jesus to baptize him, right then, with the Holy Spirit. He also asked Him for the same sign those first century Christians experienced when they were endued with power from on high.

The Lord met him almost instantly! He was dramatically and beautifully manifesting proof of surrender of his tongue, our most unruly member, to Jesus the Baptizer with the Holy Spirit.

It was just 2:45 and as John left I handed him a copy of a new book I had just finished, *You Shall Receive Power*. It was the story of my own baptism.

Two weeks later at home I was scanning the Los Angeles *Times* church page when my eye was arrested by a big display ad.

CHRIST CHURCH UNITY
Pastor, Rev. John Hinkle

Sermon Topic:
"You Shall Receive Power"
Church Service: 11 A.M.

I read on to see that Reverend Hinkle's message was to be broadcast over radio. "Hm-m-m! I wonder what in the world John will say?"

I called Virginia's mom, and told her what I had just read. "I'm going to be teaching at eleven tomorrow. Could you tune in to Hinkle's program tomorrow, Mimi? I'm curious to learn what he's going to say!"

We hurried home from church and I called Mimi for a report. She exclaimed, "He was very good—I really enjoyed Reverend Hinkle's sermon. Every bit of it was scripturally sound. You could just sense that he has had a fresh encounter with Jesus."

"Whew, what relief!" He was so new in the Spirit.

In about fifteen days, John was back on the phone again, "George, how about ministering for us here next week at our mid-week healing meeting?" When I asked him what he wanted me to talk on, he said, "Well, you could give your testimony."

"You wouldn't want me to give it all would you?" I asked.

"Anything you want to say—otherwise I wouldn't have called you," John replied.

I stood in the high mahogany lectern of the beautiful old church sharing both the story of my salvation and my baptism —nothing held back! Then I said, "Reverend Hinkle has opened up for us the big corner chapel room. If there is any-one here tonight that would like to be sure they know Jesus as Saviour, and if any of you want to know more about the Baptism with the Holy Spirit then please go on over into the chapel. I will meet with you there after the service."

The chapel was too small for all of the inquirers and about twenty had to stand outside the big doors. That cool Los Angeles night, more than ninety people in the ornate old Unity chapel prayed for forgiveness of their sins, in the Name of Jesus Christ. They acknowledged Jesus' essential work on Calvary and invited Him into their hearts. He became Lord of their lives forevermore. And some thirty stayed behind to meet Christ as Baptizer with the Holy Spirit.

God was rattling the gates of that great old denomination as He is now rattling the gates of every manner of church. Some gates may be guarded by well-meaning "defenders of the doc-trines and traditions" of the institution, but Jesus' voice out there at the gates is being heard by certain responding hearts inside of each. *And the Spirit and the bride say, Come. And let him that heareth say, Come. And let him that is athirst come. And whosoever will, let him take the water of life freely* (Revelation 22:17).

Jesus is now meeting His people in this new/old way re-gardless of the name chiseled on the front of the buildings. You see, God looks upon the hearts of men not their labels! Catholic, Epsicopalian, Presbyterian, Baptist, Quaker, Lu-theran, Plymouth Brethren, Church of Christ, and now Unity. Jesus in His fulness is now finding responsive hearts and vessels—and the remnant is growing! Now He is pouring out of His Spirit upon all flesh in these last of the last days— just as He promised in Joel and Isaiah.

A few days later came a long distance call. "This is Reverend Jonnie Coleman, pastor of Unity Temple here in Chicago. Would you be available to come to the Chicago area next month to lecture to our congregation?"

I answered enthusiastically, "It will be a pleasure, I'll be glad to come." It was an electrifying repeat of the harvest in John's church. Two courageous shepherds willing to pay a price and stick their necks out for their flock. Jesus mightily rewarded them with a harvest of harvests!

Will His wonders and His miracles ever cease! No—never! To Him be the glory and the honor forever and ever.

13

Mister Boone

"Mister Boone. Oh, Mr. Boone, please!"

The sharp-looking gal in the coral dress giggled as her hands jabbed toward his face with the program and a broken yellow pencil. They were breaking out of every aisle door now and churning through the lobby. It had now been several years since that heavenly lesson back in Philadelphia at the book-sellers' convention.

First one, and then another spotted him. The thronging started again. I had seen it many times, but it always surprised me. I think it does him, too.

"Mr. Boone, I just adored the picture. You were so dynamic in it, and it was such a *different* part! I've never seen you in anything like this. It was really inspirational. It seemed almost like a true story. But I wish you could have sung 'April Love' in it someplace. I still have my record, Oh, thank you for your autograph."

Then another tugging at the buttons on his sleeve. A pen this time, and a torn page from a magazine. "Please sign this for my daughter, Pat." Then that nervous giggle again. "Are you really Pat Boone? You look like him all right, but you're too young!" She continued, "Why, when I was a young girl, you were singing 'Love Letters in the Sand' on the Godfrey

Show. I thought you'd look a lot older by now; why, it's been years, Mr. Boone, ten or fifteen anyhow! How do you stay looking like that? That Nickey Cruz was sure mean before he got straightened out, wasn't he? I liked that scene where you preached, Pat. Thanks for your signature — my daughter will never believe it."

Shirley, Pat, Virginia and I began to press out of the lobby toward the parking lot. It was the sneak preview of *The Cross and the Switchblade* way out in a suburban theater and the regular covey of strangers moved with us toward his dark green Rolls convertible. Pat asked, "What did you think of it?"

I replied, "Well, we only got here in time to see the last half. I'm sure this picture is going to have a real impact as it runs in the theaters. There's never been anything quite like it before, has there? I heard people buzzing in the lobby about your preaching scene to those gangs near the end. I think it may be the best scene you've ever done in your whole career, Pat." And it really was outstanding.

(But I did consider to myself, however, "I wasn't impressed with the way some of it was handled. I wonder who directed this picture anyhow? Both Dave Wilkerson, as a person, and *The Cross and the Switchblade* story are masculine, and deeply spiritual." It had seemed to me that in a couple of scenes the director was trying to make Dave into the stereotyped Hollywood preacher.

I sort of wished Pat would have punched him in the nose, or something! My impression was that Dave came off once as a kind of a goody-goody preacher. That's not David Wilkerson, and it wasn't Pat! I had seen how authority and command just exude from Wilkerson. His eyes could cut down a Mafia chief!)

"How's it been doing at the box office these first several days?" I asked.

Shirley asked, "Did we tell you about that preaching scene? They had prayer on the set every day all the way through the shooting in New York. On that particular day, I had an opportunity to be with Pat for the filming. I sat way back in the dark behind the lights and felt a spirit of prayer come over me.

Through every second of that scene I was almost lost in prayer. I've never had a chance to pray quite this way for any of Pat's other pictures. That scene is good!"

Pat observed, "Maybe the picture isn't perfect technically throughout—no picture ever is. But I feel this will prove to be a great picture, even so. But to answer your question about the box office, George, I talked to the manager tonight before the screening. He told me a startling thing. The box office take from this run is the second highest for him this year. And since this is a sneak preview it didn't have the regular advertising either. The manager says that their biggest attendance was for *Sound of Music*. You know, that was the number one picture of all time, so I guess *The Cross and the Switchblade* is going to be quite successful."

"That's very good news. Congratulations! I'm so glad that we got to see part of it. I'm excited about the picture and thrilled that it's finally done." And I really meant it!

Rolling home along the Santa Ana Freeway that night, I thought back several years to my drive that summer morning through the Arroyo Seco to see Jens. We had just sold some of our Astro-Science stock and I was looking for a good place to put the money back to work. Jens was a business broker and he briefed me on a couple of deals in his portfolio, but they weren't for me.

Then he remembered, "George, you like cars don't you? You know manufacturing, and have experience getting stuff built in other countries. This deal could be made for you. Are you familiar with the Apollo car?"

"Maybe," I answered, "I think Spence Nilson may have shown me a picture of one in *Motor Trend* magazine."

Jens urged, "Come on out here, George, and I'll show you one. I'm driving an Apollo that belongs to one of the members of the New Christy Minstrels." There it was! A deep maroon color, it looked as though it wore about fifty coats of lacquer.

"It looks like a Ferrari," I said.

Jens agreed, "Yes, it does, only it's better! These bodies are made in Turino, Italy, by some of the last of the great coach craftsmen. Here are a few of the good angles on the car. It has a Buick Skylark engine and a Borg-Warner transmission. This way there aren't headaches on the major parts and service that Ferrari owners have. Better yet, a Ferrari like this costs about fourteen thousand dollars. Apollo is selling for only ten thousand. They are really making money on it, too. Are you interested?"

I mumbled, "Keep talking. I know I'm not too bright, but I am smart enough to know I don't know *anything* about building cars. A thousand must have gone bust trying to enter the luxury car field."

"Pat Boone drives an Apollo himself," Jens pointed out. "He's one of our clients. I was just talking to his manager the other day, and he says Pat is crazy about the car. Pat might be interested in buying into the company, but he said, that he wouldn't let him do it unless the management is strengthened. George, how would you like to be in business with Pat Boone?"

The next afternoon I got my first look at the man. He was sitting at his desk in the former Beverly Boulevard office. It looked a little like mine and that was kind of a surprise—for a movie star. I guess I expected it to have zebra couches, flashing lights, and white angora rugs!

But his desk looked active. There were lots of papers and folders on the top—just like my own—but there were a few clues about the man: all those framed gold records, the two thousand dollar recorder, and the photograph of him with presidents. The first time I ever saw him he was puffing on a pipe. It was the real Pat Boone, all right; I could tell by the shoes! "It's a privilege to meet you, Mr. Boone." Then he surprised me!

"Didn't you used to run the Lear operations out at the Santa Monica airport?" He began then to sell me on the Apollo. Why, he really was interested in this car deal!

We ended the meeting with my saying, "Mr. Boone, I feel

that the key to success or failure on this project lies in Italy. I don't want to put much time or money into the Apollo, and I don't think you should either—until one of us can get over there and take a hard look at the body works and the tooling." Then I continued, "I am intrigued enough though to fly over there and try to do this study for us if Jens will call the body plant in Turino. I could be in Italy next week."

Two weeks later the maid invited me into the foyer of the big French mansion on Sunset Boulevard. It was one of those bright California days, but the drapes were drawn in the living room and it was a bit dark inside. Pat sort of jogged down those winding stairs wearing some faded denim jeans, so the expensive leather jacket was a contrast. "He looks even more boyish with his hair ruffled," I thought.

As we sat in the den, I started immediately with the conclusions stemming from the Apollo research I had done in Italy the week before. I have always been conscious of the tremendous pressures of his personal schedule. It seems as though he is steadily on sixteen-hour days with thirty or so appointments. People were always lined up waiting on the phone lines or just standing around to see him.

I came right to the point. "Mr. Boone, I feel that the Apollo deal is too marginal."

He broke in immediately, "But, George, I've looked at the figures—and they're attractive! The costs on the major components are unusually favorable and their projections show nearly a two thousand dollar profit per car. But I think they are *conservative* because I know that the engine price he has included in the figures is too high. It's the best car I have ever owned in my life, and I have had several good ones. It's better than a Ferrari or a Maserati and mine has been trouble-free. It roads like an Indianapolis racer. With your experience, this company could make us both some money."

I replied, "No, my mind is made up! I have to analyze situations like this and come to my own judgment alone and apart from the emotional persuasion of the principals. I feel that the tooling for the bodies over in Italy is mickey mouse. There will never be two bodies exactly alike because of that tooling. I'm also concerned about the financial strength of the body firm. I know they can make some of these cars OK by hand, just as they have been. They can handle that, but I don't think they can build four times that many acceptable bodies per month. And I believe we would have to produce that volume to break even. This is just my own opinion."

There was a copy of a little book on the coffee table over across the room. It was a very familiar one, *The Cross and the Switchblade.* I asked, terminating the Apollo discussion, "Have you read this?"

He said, "Yes, I read it on a recent trip to Mexico City and we are negotiating for the movie rights to the story. I would like to try to do the David Wilkerson part." I sucked in my breath and then very slowly said it!

"I don't believe you can do it, Mr. Boone. But that is an outstanding book and I do feel you should go ahead and negotiate for its movie rights."

Pat was kind of surprised. "What about the David Wilkerson part? Why do you see this as difficult?"

I answered him honestly, "The very heart of the Teen Challenge story lies in the spiritual power Reverend Wilkerson has in his own life. If anyone tries just to act out his life — without having his personal experience — I don't think it will come off right. It might seem phony and I don't feel that you or the best actor in the business can really put it over on the screen. I don't think it can be done by method acting or any other technique. Anyway, I suggest that you not try it yet, at least until you know what I mean."

Suddenly the atmosphere in the room was different. Finally I really felt at ease and he seemed comfortable, too.

"Where's Mrs. Boone?" I asked.

He replied, "She's upstairs. Shirley isn't feeling well today. She really hasn't been herself since our housekeeper Eva died."

"Is that why the drapes are pulled in the house?" I inquired, and he answered, "That's part of it, I suppose."

The Cross and the Switchblade had pried off the lid and I
inquired about his own Christian life. I already knew he was a
churchman. He still had the best moral image in the business.
He was Goody-Two-Shoes in Hollywood and just becoming
obsolete due to the deteriorating movie quality. Who had a
part for the nice clean-cut American boy-next-door, even
with a rich baritone? Now it was the era of hard rock, booze,
and swingers. And audiences would laugh uncomfortably at
the stories about milk-drinking Mr. Clean from the likes of
Rickles, Martin, and all of them.

The Nashville boy came from a simple home. Pat was the
boy who had chased the family cow through the neighbors'
yards, who went to his Church of Christ meetings three times
a week. He seemed unspoiled and there was still that bend
toward wholesomeness. It remained there in his fibre even
after the thirteen million-seller gold records, the seventeen
pictures, thousands of personal appearances, and the years of
radio and TV with Ted Mack and Arthur Godfrey. Even after
hosting hundreds of his own shows, his boyish charm and
natural simplicity remained.

The handsome Beverly hillbilly from Tennessee! Great-
great-great-grandson of Daniel Boone, Pat, too, was a legend
in his own time. His name was known to millions of people
around the world, yet here he was still easy and gracious, as
though he had never fully awakened to who he really was.

Then he asked, "George, are you a Christian? What about
yourself?" He eased back in the rawhide covered rocker and
just watched me. I started slowly, sketching in the sordid essence of my early life, and then on to that point several years
earlier when I had met Christ in the church not far from Pat's
house. Then I hesitated and prayed as I stalled for time. There
seemed to be a second wind and the story went on. During
only my second meeting with the famous Mr. Boone, I un-
loaded it—all of it. Tongues and the whole thing!

While the story unfolded I was thinking to myself. "I'll never have another chance, so I had better make the most of this one now. Besides—he asked for it! He'll never want to see me again!"

"You know, Pat, *this* is David Wilkerson's 'secret weapon'— the one I hinted to you about. He has the Baptism with the Holy Spirit. That's partly why he is so bold and effective. That's what is behind the fabulous results in the Teen Challenge ministry. This is why they are having success getting heroin addicts delivered while the best of our medical field stands helpless. David Wilkerson knows Jesus Christ in a dimension that makes him a fierce and victorious warrior against the forces of darkness! I feel that you will need the same encounter that Wilkerson had before you'll be ready to adequately play Dave in the movie."

I didn't see or hear from Pat again for four months. During that time the Apollo had collapsed. Pat had evidently been impressed with my judgment on the project, but only God had done it! The Lord had given me wisdom in this matter, and through it came grace and favor in the eyes of Mr. Boone. Sometimes the wisdom of the Lord makes us look wise to other people!

Then there were intermittent calls. "This is Pat—can you come over for a few minutes? We've run across a business deal and I'd like to get your reaction."

By this stage of my life, both my work and the years in California had brought me in contact with many of the movie crowd. I had developed a thing about them. Many of them seemed like strutting peacocks, and selfish demanding showboats to me. There was an aura of phoniness all dressed up in Christian Dior and Sy Devore "sheep's clothing." The spirit of showbiz kind of made me sick, and it had almost eliminated our theater going. I had seen too much of the fake people that perform before fake props. Many seemed to be craning around wherever they were, hoping people would look at them.

There's a big·Prince of Satan whose very seat is Hollywood.

He has pulled the strings and played the tune to which many of the entertainment people dance! Oh, they performed to his whistle all right—sometimes, I have felt that they would sell their souls for a single credit line. This evil spirit of show business has performed before our great nation, and has played its dreadful part in bringing our country to its present posture— staggering like a sniveling giant. This is an enemy of my Lord and I have made God's enemies my enemies.

There were only a handful of stars that I had personally known in all those years who were authentic Christians. I had met only these few not possessed by showbizitis—that spirit that keeps them forever acting whether they are on cameras or just sitting in a restaurant. Most of the rest seemed lost in the unreality, no longer able to tell truth from fiction. So it's no wonder that the Christian community looks at every star that talks about religion with a "We'll just wait and watch you for a while, Mr. Big."

And so a deep respect began to grow for this fellow Boone. It grew in spite of the fact that he, too, was an actor. I began to sense that he wasn't just acting, and it took me awhile to see his many facets. This wasn't just some emptyheaded singer. He had graduated magna cum laude from Columbia even while he was cutting his first gold record. He has a phenomenal memory. One time I hadn't seen Pat for a whole year and his first words were, "George, you're combing your hair different!" He was right, but how could he remember one haircut? He had probably seen a hundred thousand people since we last met. And his ability to get things done is sometimes hard to believe. Last month, we saw him tape, not just one, but five major television shows—in one afternoon!

Then there was the time Harald Bredesen, Pat, and I were invited to do a TV program at Faith Center in Glendale. It was to be kind of a seminar on the serious crises in America — spiritual, political, moral.

Harald and I spent a great deal of time writing material that God gave us for the program scheduled for that night. It became *pages* of script. One-third Harald was to give; one-third for Pat; and the rest I was to present. This complex message later became a best seller entitled *The Solution to Crisis-America.*

Harald and I worked over the script carefully ahead of time, and then the people started to come. Seventeen hundred started to jam into an auditorium designed for seven hundred. We had prearranged with Pat to get there one hour ahead so he could go over all of the material that he was to do. He was early that night—for Pat, that is. The preliminaries had already begun in the auditorium and there wasn't enough time left when he arrived to go over his portion. The script was intricate—enough for a full one-hour broadcast.

Pat was breathing hard and said, "I'm a little late. Can I get a look at the material?" He took the *seven minutes* he had! Seven whole minutes to scan the hour long, three-part script. I was shook! Harald and I had labored over our homework ahead of time; now he would probably blow it because of his lateness! Didn't he have a watch?

Pat stepped before the cameras and opened his mouth. Out of it flowed a brilliant presentation on American history—the spiritual fibre that made America great—and all of it was laced with Scriptures. Pat not only worked in the material we had assembled that weekend for him, but he added to and improved on it extemporaneously. Seven minutes preparation!

The audience roared as he sat down and that sound track was so good that it has become a record album. It stirred not only the Christian community, but the president too. George Romney took it to him, and Pat soon received an inspired *thank you* from the White House. Seven minutes! What could this be? Why had God built so many talents and features and facets into one man?

Some weeks earlier Shirley and Pat had taken us to a Hollywood Celebrity basketball game. It was one of those affairs where a bunch of the big names get out on the floor and awkwardly run around in a clumsy caricature of the sport for charity. It was the celebrities that people paid to see. They don't expect athletic prowess, and they don't get it!

Mr. White Buck Shoes hadn't been shaped into the image of a John Wayne by the Hollywood propaganda mills—just Mr. Nice with the good looks and the great voice. And somehow you didn't think about him as six-feet tall and athletic. But there he was, out there on the floor with Pat Paulsen, Jim Garner, and friends dribbling like Jerry West on a driving layup—and scoring!

He could even write—two books—two hits! *Twixt Twelve and Twenty* and now *A New Song*. Both promptly shot onto the best-seller lists.

We've recently seen tears flow from hundreds of eyes as he sang "He Touched Me." We've watched scores come to Christ as this man has spoken with the power of a Wesley. We have witnessed a thousand young people deeply stirred as he shared Christ with them at Ralph Wilkerson's Melodyland Church.

I suppose we'll never really know this fellow. Few are aware of the real scope of his achievements, least of all, himself. God is up to something with this life! I was beginning to suspect what that might be.

14

A Shaft of Light

Pat in trouble? Yes, and it seemed to be coming from every-where! All of his life the good things had fallen his way, and now everything seemed to be coming unglued. It was obvious now that career management by some of his former agents had been faulty over the past years. Pat had never been entirely happy with the entertainment business, and he had, in fact, prepared to be a teacher. His active mind increasingly longed to find escape into something more satisfying.

Business deals fascinated him, but he had gotten poor advice on first one thing and then another. So maybe he did have a flaw after all. He seemed ready to believe every person who came along with a deal. The most militant of optimists, he always wanted to get in on every opportunity. It was as though he was afraid to lose out on something that might later turn out to be a good deal—like the Apollo—or Telequick.

Pat had asked me to fly back to Indiana to look over a new business that was being developed there. He had already invested in it and had already made television spots backing the Telequick concept with his own reputation. Back I came again with a rather depressing report on its prospects. It was a fine and unique approach to TV service, but they lacked the management and the big funding that would be needed to put it over.

I counseled, "Don't put any more money into this thing, Pat. You may lose what you have already put up." It was the same old story. A man with MENSA calibre IQ, but vulnerable in business matters for some unexplainable reason.

It may have all begun with the disintegration of American tastes—that sudden demand for filth, depravity, and perversion on our screens. It left Boone stranded awkwardly on the rocks of decency as that black tide flowed in. One of his agents panicked when overnight the market had evaporated for a wholesome genius.

Then perhaps the most costly professional advice of all— probably unconsciously done—but the net result was still: "Sell your soul, Pat; become relevant to the times. Change your pattern—you've got to conform to today's market." Almost Mephistophelian!

"*State Fair* and Debbie Reynolds are obsolete. Get with it, son! The world has moved on. Wake up! You're an actor, and you've still got a name. Maybe a Pat Boone drunk scene—or take off your clothes, Pat, and crawl into bed with that sexy actress right before the cameras. There, that'll do it! It shouldn't be too hard to smash that old obsolete Pat Boone image with just a few more smart moves. How about the *Yellow Canary?* or maybe one or two more even more daring?"

He just couldn't pull it off. His heart wasn't in it, and he failed. Praise God, he failed! There wasn't a market any more for the late Mr. Clean and now he was a flop as the new Mr. X. He was too dirty now for the clean market, and too clean for the new leering, lustful market.

Shoddy advice had almost consumed the twenty million dollars earned by the young man. And as the view from the French mansion grew darker, Pat and I were seeing each other a bit more each year. We talked about these new problems occasionally, but mostly we just talked about the Lord. Pat had begun to listen to Bible Voice tapes over his stereo in the new Ferrari. He said they were a blessing at this difficult stage.

Virginia and I had met Shirley only once before. It was a

long and pleasant evening at the Boone home to meet some old friends of theirs. That Shirley — she is something else again! She is the high-strung, handsome daughter of Red Foley, King of Country Music and gospel artists. Red may have invented the Nashville sound. But eternity may show, too, that Red will be known even longer for the four daughters he sired than for "Peace in the Valley."

Maybe it was her voice that captivated us — we didn't know. She sounds like Jo Stafford, only better. But there was an intensity — almost a desperation — in Shirley. Shirley was carrying a load right then.

Pat and Shirley had married while they were just kids while attending Lipscomb, a Church of Christ college. Shirley was famous in Nashville as Red Foley's girl. She and Pat eloped and moved to Texas and the coin of God took a funny bounce. Now she was Mrs. Pat Boone, with four pretty girls, but here again came some of those same pressures she had known as a child in the Foley household! Wouldn't it ever let up?

A few days later Shirley phoned. "Hello, George, could you and Virginia come over to our house for breakfast tomorrow morning? An old Church of Christ friend of ours from Fresno has just come in. Merlyn Lund is a contractor who says he has had the same experience that you told Pat about in your own life. I think it would be helpful to Merlyn if you would come over and encourage him. He's going through a lot of persecution in his church right now. Can you come?"

Shirley was as fidgety that next morning as she usually was in those days — maybe more so. She didn't touch her breakfast and she talked ninety-miles-an-hour. Shirley really was suffering from all these new pressures in their lives! Pat was down in Texas that day making a series of personal appearances.

Shirley had been standing on the sidelines over the past year or so and just watched as Pat submitted to advice to dirty up his image. She was spiritually sensitive and had a heart for God. After maybe an hour, first Merlyn, then Virginia and I turned to Shirley as if we had rehearsed it all before.

We began to share the wonders of the Spirit-filled life with

her, and the Scriptures just started to flow. We began to challenge Shirley personally, but with deep compassion.

"Shirley, *have ye received the Holy Ghost since ye believed?*" (Acts 19). If ever there was a person who would bene-
fit from God's power from on high, it was Shirley, right then.
If ever there was a time when someone needed all God had
for them it was Shirley Boone that day.

Quickly I went through the highlights in the Bible concerning Jesus the Baptizer. Then we got up from the table and I
said, "Shirley, I think we're supposed to leave you alone now.
You know all that's really essential about the Baptism with the
Holy Spirit. Why don't you go up to your bedroom after we go
and just talk to the Lord alone. Your life will be transformed by
this new dimension of the Holy Spirit. You don't need anybody
else around to receive and Isaiah tells us, *This is the rest
wherewith ye may cause the weary to rest; and this is the refreshing* (28:12).

I continued, "Nobody laid hands on those Christians on the
day of Pentecost or there at Cornelius's house when the Spirit
fell on the Gentiles for the first time. Only two are essential in
this, Jesus the Baptizer—and you. Just ask Him to baptize you
with the Holy Spirit. Surrender as you do and open your mouth
and start praising God, but not in English this time, please."

Virginia and I headed through Coldwater Canyon toward
home that morning. Shortly after we arrived there, the phone
rang.

"It's me. It's Shirley. It happened. He did it! Praise the Lord
—I can't believe it! George, it's like a dream! I haven't felt this
way since I was a little girl. Jesus is so wonderful. Oh, I love
Him!" Then she said, "I couldn't wait 'til I called Pat down in
Texas."

I stammered, "You told him? Golly! What did he say?"

Shirley laughed, "Why, Pat said, 'Honey, I'm so happy for
you! I can tell somehow this is real. I'm anxious to hear every
detail. Maybe it won't be long now until something happens
to me, too.'"

I was relieved. "Did he really say that, Shirley?"

"Yes, he knows. I told him everything and he wasn't mad. Thank you both for coming over this morning. Now I know it wasn't just for Merlyn, after all. I guess the Lord wanted to do something for me, too, and I'm so happy."

From that day we never saw the old Shirley Boone again. She was a changed person and wonderfully new. The tension and that jitteriness were gone. There was quietness and a new beauty—the new sound of a softly running fountain in her spirit.

It wasn't all good though! It was only a few days until Shirley started to steal! She would sneak out into the garage and get Pat's Bible tapes. Pat's hunger for the Word of God had now infected Shirley, too.

Over the next weeks the forces of God began to surge through every fibre of the optimistic Mr. Boone. Seemingly, capricious forces collided in his mind. The rigid doctrines of his beloved denomination were coming into collision with the new spiritual currents around him. And at the same time his own career and financial future were being shaken.

His loving Father in Heaven seemed to have spoken. "Heat up the furnace of his life seven times more! Burn away the false optimism, self-confidence, security of career, excess finances, complacency, and every imperfect doctrine of men." The prayers of his godly father and mother, the A. A. Boones, down in Nashville, were finally being answered. And Pat's own prayers for more of God were also being answered, but in a strange and terrifying manner! A wise and merciful Father was now plowing up Boone's back in preparation for dropping His seeds of Heaven.

It began to go something like this:

"Good morning, Pat. Sorry we can't send you those checks we owe you yet. Can you make another trip for us? We have to step up sales immediately! We need all our funds here in the business, but we'll try to pay you what we owe you soon. This thing is really going great though! How soon can you go out for us, Pat? We need your image to get us over this temporary hump."

Then another, "Hello, Pat. No, we didn't make it with ABC. They gave it to some new fellow. I think they said his name is Tom Jones or some name like that. No, I don't think it was our price. I don't know whether he sings or not. They wanted some sexy guy to fit the new image." On and on the new blows came.

It was rough! His loving Father was, however, dropping a few good little clues along his path during those same furnace weeks. One night Pat overheard Shirley praying softly in her new language. He did a doubletake! "Shirley, can you say that again."

"What, Pat?"

"Were you praying in tongues, honey?"

Shirley answered, "Yes, I was, did you hear me?"

"Please try to say it again — what you just said." Then Shirley started again and Pat stopped her.

"Say it slower, honey." She slowed down and prayed with the Spirit again and then again.

"Shirley — Do you know what you're saying?" For all of his four years in high school Pat had selected Latin for his language credits. God had seen to it. Pat knew his wife never spoke nor understood a single word of Latin, but now Shirley was praising the Lord of Heaven in beautiful, flawless *Latin* — magnifying God!

Yes, Jesus was there with them too in their besieged French mansion. It was a glorious, jolting miracle, and Pat knew he had been the recipient of a dramatic display of one of God's gifts! It was a deep encouragement in the midst of those troubles.

But this much trouble could burn up a man! Wouldn't it be destructive? It was as though the Lord of Heaven had spoken yet again: "Heat it up still more. Burn the dross. Burn *all* of it, but touch not a gram of the gold." Our Lord doesn't waste pages of His Bible to tell a single story that isn't still relevant for His children today!

Recall wealthy Job watching his own material security disintegrating around him—then his body dreadfully stricken.
Along came his religious friends, "Job, there must be some
kind of secret sin in your life. It's obvious you are out of God's
will. He is punishing you! God has turned His back on you,
and you're a has-been! Maybe you were just lucky to get all
these riches in the first place. Repent of your sins. Can't you
see, Job? God doesn't love you anymore."

Even Job's wife turned on him and said, *Curse God, and die*
(Job 2:9). Oh, no—God loved Job as much as any man alive.
God knew Job's heart and He also knew his limits. Job passed
his test when he sobbed, *Though he slay me, yet will I trust
in him. . . .* (13:15). He forgave his friends and the tide started
to turn. Job's possessions and his reputation were restored
right before their eyes.

Now Pat was sitting on the top of his own heap. *Though he
slay me, yet will I trust in him.* My intercom buzzer sounded
and its light flashed. It was Evelyn, my secretary, "Mr. Boone
is calling."

"Yes, this is George. How are you, Pat? It's nice to hear
from you. No, I'm not too busy. I was just getting ready to
dictate some letters. How was your trip?"

Pat replied, "Fine. Listen George, what are you doing tonight? I think I may be ready. Could we get together somewhere to study about the Holy Spirit? I feel a real need for
some prayer time, too. I don't want to foul up your own plans,
George—if you have something going, we can do it another
time. Maybe Virginia and Shirley could join us, too."

"Tonight is clear for me," I agreed. "Why don't you come
over to our house—but I don't think the girls are supposed to
be with us tonight. Let's just spend an hour or two alone with
our Bibles. Would seven or seven-thirty be too early for you?"

Pat and I sat down side by side on the green couch, looking
over toward the crackling fireplace in our den. I always liked
that room; it was so warm and friendly with its wood paneling,
and its beamed ceiling slanting skyward like a ski lodge. This

was just about where old Doctor Follette had stood to teach us at his wonderful home meetings. How he had fed our souls that week he was here!

Both of our Bibles were opened and the minutes flew as our fingers riffled through the pages. The Lord's own shafts of light were awakening our understanding as He spoke to us from His Word that night. From Isaiah and Joel, and flashes from here and there through the Gospel. Then Acts and Romans, both of the Corinthians, and finally a last burst from James.

My own spirit was purring from the wonderful Bread of Heaven—His Word. It is ever fresh and the only fully satisfying food. Pat declared, "That was really something! Shall we pray now?"

"If you feel ready and want to—why don't you ask Jesus to meet you?"

"Shall we kneel?" Pat asked.

"No, why don't you sit in that chair over there and be comfortable. Just close your eyes and talk to Him. I can sense you're ready, and Jesus will meet you now if you ask Him to."

The boyish-looking celebrity with many personal characteristics of a David started to talk to his Lord. He asked Jesus to baptize him with the Holy Spirit and give him a new prayer language, just as He had for the Apostle Paul, those early Christians on the day of Pentecost, and also those at Ephesus and at Cornelius's house.

Pat asked for his own new tongue that he might know that Jesus had endued him with His power from on High, and that he might have it for his own private prayer times. Then he sat back quietly. Nothing happened. The clock was ticking on. More seconds and still nothing. He was just sitting there in the black teakwood chair waiting and hoping that the Lord would work in him—sitting there alone with Jesus. There was a gentle quietness. Not a sound came—no emotion here.

Maybe forty seconds had gone by when a thought came to me—an unusual one. Was it coming from that still small voice?

I waited and prayed trying to test it in my heart. It persisted, so I got up and walked to his chair. I said quietly with one hand on his shoulder, "Pat, why don't you raise your hands and just sing to Jesus—but not in English?" Never had I thought about anyone *singing* with the Spirit as I had prayed with others before for the baptism.

Immediately it started! No one ever heard this singer pour out such a song! The melody was intricate, exquisite, soaring, and then fluttering down and around. The words were distinct, and they seemed to fit perfectly with the melody. It went on and on, and now he was quietly walking with his hands lifted. Back and forth across the room. How I would like to be able to play that song back again! I know it pierced the ceiling shooting heavenward to bring fragrance and delight to his Heavenly Father. There was a sense of praise, adoration, worship, of magnifying God. The deep of his spirit was calling to the deep in God's great heart!

Pat drove home across Coldwater Canyon that night bearing a new handprint from his Jesus on his soul!

15

Miracle of the Oaks

Relaxing there in the hot whirlpool in Palm Springs I got to chuckling to myself; He *is* funny! Koala bears, anteaters, monkeys, giraffes, and pups. He has the ultimate sense of humor and He sure isn't dead. I love my Lord, not only because of His might and power, but also His glorious sense of humor.

I recalled the time when that preacher came to the Boones' after word got out about their new trouble—the Holy Spirit. The "defenders of the doctrine" were implementing their rescue plan so no need to worry about the Boones anymore. They had set in motion a great strategy and one of their finest soldiers was dispatched to save the Boones. The brilliant young pastor of Northside Church was sent—a perfect selection, in every way. Not only had Reverend Dennis proved himself in his theological training, but also as the faithful pastor of the big church. Dean Dennis is an outstanding Bible scholar and a student of the Greek language.

He stayed all day as a guest at the big Sunset Boulevard mansion and the air was filled with talk. Reverend Dennis said he would like to meet the fellow who was passing along this teaching.

"How about trying to set up a Bible study tonight?" Shirley

volunteered brightly. "We could call in some friends. Then
you can sit in and hear for yourself how it goes. This way you
can meet him and ask him questions yourself."

That night, sixteen of us sat around the big round table in
Pat Boone's den for three hours reading and rereading Scriptures from the Book. There was not much talk about experiences—the Word was doing its own talking. Not too much
here for the church emissary to battle—you can't fight His
Word, can you?

The bright young preacher left—a failure in his mission, as
other men might view it. Once back home this Bible scholar
began hunting through the Book and through his library and
through his Greek lexicon. Reverend Dennis was searching for
flaws in that round-table session.

Some weeks later, the same young emissary, Dean Dennis,
sat in that same high-ceilinged wood-paneled room in our
Van Nuys house disturbing the neighborhood! Dean had just
met Jesus as Baptizer with the Holy Spirit himself and in one
of the most beautiful encounters! The self-assured young
Pharisee with his polished manners was magnifying God now
at a high decibel level!

My sunshine dreaming went back to the time Harald
Bredesen and a business friend, Paul Lincoln, had driven me
over to Pasadena to meet their friends, the Lazarians. Steve
Lazarian and his wife stood outside the office of their construction business. The place seemed too big for the few
people working there.

While we waited to leave for lunch, they were sharing with
us. It was exciting to hear how the Lazarians' engineering and
construction business was dedicated to God, and how they
used the building for weekend Bible studies.

"But money is a problem, right now and we are in a tight
place," they told us. It was a real crisis time for their business.
They explained how they had spent money to prepare and
submit many bids on construction jobs around Southern Cal-

ifornia. Every customer had in recent times had a different excuse, and none of their bids had materialized into a job now for weeks. The stories had a pattern.

Their customers would say, in effect, "We have your bid and it's good. We are ready to go ahead on our new building, but the banks don't have the money to loan right now, so we can't start the job." One after another of these expensive proposals had melted into nothingness!

"Look," the Lazarians said, "just look at the empty drafting tables, but our Lord is good and He will somehow bring us through this. But please remember us in your prayers, if you think about it."

Now, it was time for lunch and we were walking along between their building and the parking lot. We were moving along in a loose, strung-out group. It wasn't until right then that I responded to a persistent thought—one of those strong ones! After another twenty-five or thirty steps, I called to the ones ahead, "Say, could we take a minute for prayer before we go on to lunch? Could we all go back inside for a minute? I feel we are to pray for Steve's business right now."

We turned around and all filed back into the building. As Steve opened the door to a room he remarked, "We can pray in here—it's not too hard to find an empty office right now." We stood there for a few minutes holding hands and praying,

"Dear Lord, we cry out to You, in behalf of Steve's company. We bind you, Satan from any further interference in the bids and finances of this business! It is written that what we bind on earth in the Name of Jesus, shall be bound in Heaven, and we now bind every spirit and every circumstance coming against Steve's business and in Jesus Name we right now loose those contracts! We thank You Lord that You said if two of us shall agree concerning *anything* in Your Name that it shall be done. We now agree together for victory here. Thank You, for hearing and answering our prayers."

We had only taken a couple of minutes from that luncheon schedule. Two weeks later, Harald called. "Have you heard about Lazarian's business?"

"No, I haven't."

"The employees are telling an 'in' joke over at his place. Their business is just flooding in now and they are kidding Steve and telling him to get a hold of that fellow over in Northridge and tell him to stop praying!"

Then my mind drifted on to the scary episode with the Oaks, and its humorous twist at the end.

I think it was at our last home meeting before we moved from the Sunnyslope house. I was standing up making the introductions when Pat and Shirley came in. They were pressing through the rows of people toward two empty chairs near the back. Never before nor since have I seen Pat look like that. He wasn't handsome right then, and he didn't look healthy, happy, or young. He looked tired and older! What in the world had happened to him? I continued to talk while my eyes followed them. "Maybe he and Shirley had a spat on the way over," I mused. But that wasn't like them.

The meeting was finally over, and five of us were standing near the corner of the pool out in our backyard—Harold Mc-Naughton, Mel Taylor, Pat, Harald, and myself. Shirley had been detained inside by some people, and Pat was explaining to us how he had dreaded to come tonight. He just wanted to go somewhere and hide from everything and everybody. It had been one of the most humiliating days of his life.

The Oakland Oaks basketball franchise had been bought and financed by Pat and one of his sportsmen friends. The Oaks were leading their own league that night. Basketball Star Rick Barry gave them class on the floor, and supercoach Alex Hannum class on the bench. It was a truly great ABA team—except at the box office.

The Oakland citizens were staying away from the Oaks games in record numbers, and now the franchise was losing about a thousand dollars a day. And the bloodletting has been going on for a couple of years.

Pat had somehow signed the Bank of America loan papers made out in such a way that the bank could hold Pat solely responsible for the teams huge bank borrowings in the event of trouble. Oh, yes, the other owner had signed, too, but the bank had apparently found that his collateral was too small. Only Boone had the assets to make good the bank's big loan, they felt.

For a year now, Pat's business experts had been canvassing the whole country contacting every wealthy sportsman that they could think of in an effort to sell the Oaks. They had a tiger by the tail! Some buyers had come close, but one after another they had turned their backs when they saw the losses and the overhanging bank debt!

That very day the dreaded letter from the Bank of America loan officer had come! It read (in essence):

Dear Mr. Boone:
This is our final notice. The Oakland Oaks Corporation now owes the bank more than two million dollars. Our loan committee has asked me to notify you immediately that we have no alternative but to hold you personally responsible for immediate repayment of this entire loan.
If you have already sent your check just ignore this notice.

"It was almost funny," Pat said, "Like a notice from the telephone company. You know — one of those collection forms for a seven-dollar payment six days past due: 'If your check is in the mail, just ignore this notice.'"

Little did they know how much of a toll the land project had already taken of Pat's assets. And the Internal Revenue Service a couple of weeks earlier had also sent notice that his previous years' tax returns were to be reaudited. Pat didn't have two million dollars lying around. (Who does?) This seemed to be *it* for superstar Boone. The Tennessee boy who earned twenty million had finally gotten his superoptimism deflated.

When Pat told us about the bank my mind and spirit were momentarily fear-paralyzed! We had been praying about the Oaks problem over recent weeks, but it was apparent we hadn't prayed through. We suddenly felt Pat's burden as if it were our own, and that's the way it's supposed to be among members of the Body of Christ.

The victories and the joys of one Christian can be felt and thrilled to by other Christians. And the problems, sicknesses, sorrows, and tragedies of another can also be felt so acutely by those sensitive to Christ's Spirit. *Bear ye one another's burdens, and so fulfil the law of Christ*, it says in Galatians 6:2.

There wasn't a joining of hands — we threw our arms around each other and hugged tightly together in a silent huddle. Then it started:

"Dear Lord, we have a terrible emergency here. Please help Pat in this impossible situation. People are just hearing that Pat and Shirley have made Jesus Christ the very Lord of their lives and that they have now received the baptism. Many of these people will think that Pat and Shirley's new dedication to Christ came only because of their emotional reaction to this Oaks financial problem. Some may think the Boones just grasped at a straw of religious comfort because of this financial debacle. Please, Lord, don't let the true pure reason for their new surrender to You be clouded by letting this happen. We pray right now for victory. We ask that You send a mighty, a massive, and an immediate miracle to solve this Oaks problem. We pray this dear Father in the Name of Jesus Christ. Amen."

Yes, it really was sort of humorous — but not until it was over! Within forty-eight hours of that pool-side prayer a man (never approached by the experts) suddenly appeared — someone Pat never met and still hasn't met to this day. He flew from Washington, D.C. to California where he spent several hours at the Oaks' office and then with the Bank of America. This man, Earle Foreman, purchased the Oakland Oaks Basketball team and moved it to Washington. He still doesn't know that he flew across the country that day on a mission motivated by the God of Heaven Himself. Mr. Foreman became God's answer to the prayers of five hugging men around a pool twenty-five hundred miles away!

Then I recalled the time a few years back when Pat was nearly trapped! It was the very next morning after Pat had prayed with Harald up in the Hollywood Hills. Pat had just told God that He was more important than his entire career.

Harald and I rolled up the Boone drive that morning just as Pat was walking toward his car. He greeted us and told us he was on his way to sign one of the most lucrative recording contracts ever—with Tetragramaton!

I said, "Pat you can't do this. Have you prayed about it?" He looked a bit miffed at my meddling.

I reminded him, "These people just released that nude album cover with John Lennon and Yoko Ono! Pat, you mustn't be unequally yoked." Harald reminded Pat of his new commitment to God just the day before.

Pat went back into the house and stalled the contract signing meeting to gain time for more thought and prayer. Several days later he called a meeting of all the top brass of this big recording firm and gave them his new Christian testimony. He also announced that for this reason he simply couldn't sign this lucrative contract with them.

Only months later this same firm collapsed and shook the whole industry! Pat's obedience to God's Word had saved him from wiping out years from his recording career by becoming yoked for the five years of that contract—with a corpse!

16

Jesus and the Giant

I fiddled with my pen while listening to Reverend Jack Stiles. He was hitting me in a couple of sensitive spots!

If it had been boring I might have thought I was just day-dreaming. (That happens to me sometimes when it shouldn't.) My mind started drifting, "Wilt Chamberlain! Hmm! He was hurt wasn't he? I wonder if he's a Christian? I guess not, at least I never heard that he is. No—I guess he probably isn't."

I got hold of myself and latched on again to Reverend Stiles's good message, then again: "Wilt. They say he will never play again, I guess the Lakers are finished this year. They've got to have him in there! Dr. Kerlin, the team physician, is concerned about this kind of injury, since Wilt's legs are so long and thin for his mammoth stature. Seven feet, one and one-half inches! Wow! How does he ever get through doors and where does he find beds to sleep in when the team is traveling?

"This kind of injury usually leaves an athlete finished for life! Sometimes, if they're real young, they will heal again. I wonder how old Wilt is anyway? Maybe thirty or thirty-three years, I guess. All the writers seem to feel it's *over* for him.

"What's that Lord? You'll heal him!"

Suddenly I knew it wasn't just daydreaming—I was sitting up straight now! I wasn't trying to follow the sermon at all.

"Give him the Gospel? A healing of his leg? That's an exciting thought! But Wilt scares me — even on TV." I was back to the sermon again, clicking my pen nervously, and Virginia nudged me.

Now I started to pray consciously in my mind. My eyes were open, and I suppose it looked like I was listening.

"Lord, these thoughts about Wilt Chamberlain are so incongruous, but I don't want to chance ignoring them in case it's You. Is this You bringing these ideas to my mind? If it isn't, why am I thinking of Chamberlain? I've never met him and I don't know anyone that has. I don't know where Wilt lives or even if he's out of the hospital yet. Please help me, Lord. I must sort this out. I don't want to mess around with some foolish idea, but I wouldn't want to say no to You, either. If this is You, please confirm it somehow."

Nothing would dispel this preoccupation! It was as though the Lord was saying, "If you will go and tell Wilt Chamberlain about Me, I will heal his leg, and he will play basketball again."

The next morning I finished my report to Pat on a business matter and then I put down my folder. "Pat, do you have another minute or two? I had the wildest thing happen to me in church yesterday morning." Starting at the beginning, I told him what had happened.

Near the end of my story, he began to lean forward and seemed restless. Finally he broke in, "Guess who I'm going to see tonight?"

"Don't tell me — Wilt Chamberlain. Who else! You aren't really, are you? You never told me that you knew Chamberlain." I was astounded.

Pat said, "I've only met him once, but some of us are getting ready for the Celebrity Charity basketball game. Wilt's on crutches now, and he's promised to be our coach. I'm not sure he'll make it, but he promised, so I suppose he will. This could be God, George!"

We prayed together and then Pat said, "How do you think we ought to handle it? I could phone him and see if he would be willing to get together with us sometime." I asked Pat if he had Wilt's private number and he replied, "No, but I'll see if my secretary can track it down for us." He picked up the phone and dialed her.

We sat there brainstorming this unfolding plot involving The Stilt. Most sportsmen agree that Wilt Chamberlain could have been a superstar in just about any sport he chose. He could probably have been the boxing champion of the world because of his strength and reach. Then, too, what a defensive tackle he would make for the Packers! Imagine Roman Gabriel trying to pass with Wilt's arms making like ten-foot windmills before Gabriel's face?

"When I get Wilt, what do you think we should tell him?" asked Pat, "Shall I just invite him to come over to the house to meet a friend? I don't suppose we can tell him what we really want to talk about, can we? He might not come."

I thought about it and then said, "No, let's unload the whole story on him! If this idea is just something out of my own mind, Wilt won't come anyway, and that's what we want too. If, however, this really was the Lord speaking, he'll meet us regardless of how we ask him. He'll want to come somehow, so let's just play it straight."

That night the three of us sat around Pat's big stone fireplace as Wilt's king-size cast rested on the ottoman.

Wilt was simply great! Extremely intelligent, warm and attentive. Pat said, "Wilt, someone, somewhere is praying for you and the signals bounced all the way to George's church. Do you know of anyone that would be praying for you like this?"

Wilt said, "It's my mom, she's a Christian! It's probably her." We talked about the wonderful works of God that evening, and about God's Son, Jesus Christ. The Gospel had a full hearing and the big man sat alive and responsive under its light. We shared about mighty King Saul, head and shoulders above all his people and how Saul had eventually wasted his own opportunity with God. How I wished that night my ability to represent Christ was greater! I loved this man as much as anyone I had ever met, and wanted the very best for him through time and all eternity.

Finally we had been sitting around a couple of hours and it was time to go. Wilt got up awkwardly and started for his Bentley parked outside.

I said, "Wilt, remember that the Lord indicated that He would heal your leg if we would share what we have with you tonight. Would you mind very much waiting for just a minute? Is it all right . . . if we pray for you?"

Wilt nodded and said, "Sure, go ahead."

As I stood to lay hands on his knee, it seemed like I had to reach up!

"Dear Heavenly Father, In the Name of Jesus Christ, heal Wilt's leg and also help him to ponder these things we have talked about tonight. Please perform Your own miracle now in this torn knee. The experts say it's hopeless, but with You all things are possible. In the Name of Jesus, heal him! and we also pray that You will do it in time for Wilt to play again — yet this season."

He left, sitting in the back seat of the Bentley, with that long leg over the folded down seat and his foot resting near the dashboard. Just before the car pulled away, I said, "Wilt, this isn't going to be an instantaneous total healing. We feel that the Lord wants to give you a little quiet time to think about these things. But God has already started healing you and you will be in the play-offs this year!"

Wilt smiled and said, "I hope so! Thanks for the prayer." The car pulled away.

It was five months before I ever talked to Wilt again. He was thinking about jetting back with Pat Boone for the "Honor America Day" rally on the Washington mall.

"Wilt, it's great to hear your voice again," I said. "You were just sensational in the play-offs! I read in the paper how hard you worked out in the gym to strengthen your knee, but don't you think your mending was sort of a joint venture between you and Jesus?"

The big man laughed and replied, "Considering that long lay-off, the nature of that injury, and my age, it's hard to explain my comeback. I have privately felt that my performance in the play-offs was probably the best of my entire career! Yes, George, I believe that God did touch my body, and I hope that you and Pat and I can get together again for another session sometime soon."

17

Treasures from Life's Valleys

There was the crackle of high-grade stationery as the letter was slit open. I read it quickly; it said (in essence):

Dear George:
That income we committed to Bible Voice earlier is hereby cancelled and the $4000 will not be paid. There will be no future payments to Bible Voice. As you know, George, there have been many new factors that have come up here since the project started.

Bible Voice has received some benefits from the resale of the product as our distributor, but this hasn't been as profitable as we had both hoped at the beginning due to unexpected developments since we started. Therefore, the income promised must now be eliminated. Even though we put this in writing to you, I'm sure you realize that our situation has changed since we worked out the arrangements. I am sorry, but I trust you will understand.

Thank you for the part you played in getting this project started, and also for your own investment of time and expenses. We hope that as you sell the product as our distributor that this profit will prove, in time, to make it all worth while.

Sincerely yours,

The fury in me heated to a wrath in seconds and, as I struck the desk with the flat of my hand, the letter opener flew across the room! "Oh no, Lord! Not again!"

The accounts payable to our own suppliers were now running behind, and we had counted heavily on this money that was so clearly due us. To keep its bills to a minimum, Bible Voice had already borrowed from the proceeds of some stock Virginia and I had just sold to pay our own personal taxes. The shocking letter that just arrived came from a close Christian acquaintance—a fine Christian brother who headed a work of many years' standing and one known and highly respected for his outstanding work. I knew (I thought) that I always could count on him to keep his word! It had been comforting to have this agreement in writing, however, just to help us remember the ground rules of participation on the project.

Every fleshly thing flared up in me and I started to spout off to the Lord, "It's a merry-go-round with some of these people, and it seems like I can't get off of it. You just can't let this happen to me again! This can break us; you *know*, Lord, that our payroll is due tomorrow! I felt I could count on this brother, or I wouldn't have taken our personal tax money to tide Bible Voice over. How will we ever pay our own taxes now and how about the company bills? Your Word says, *Owe no man anything* . . . (Romans 13:8). We can't fulfill this Scripture if You don't keep Your own children fair toward us."

I felt like just giving up! Momentarily I was sick and tired of trying to operate in the Christian realm. Satan was having a field day in me, and I was indulging in self-pity like a spoiled kid. Quitting this realm and going back into the manufacturing business again full time sounded wonderful right then. "Sometimes it seemed you could trust people of the world more," I thought. I had been depressed to find that some believers seemed to have a different set of rules when they come to deal with another Christian.

They just wouldn't think of doing something like this to

their bank or Sears Roebuck, yet some don't seem to mind fudging a little with another Christian!

"Is that what You're trying to tell me Lord? That You *want* me to leave this Christian work now? Maybe that is what You are trying to show me. Perhaps I should change my present ministry and go back to industry full time. Maybe we then could better support the missionaries, Teen Challenge and other needy ministries. Is that it, Lord?"

Believe me, I was *mad!* The enemy had really gotten to me and I was scolding God and indulging my ego. The "old" man in me was out again!

When I was a little boy, my big brother liked to hold me and pound right on the same spot with one knuckle extended. That spot got real sore in a hurry, and it would hurt more and more as he hammered in the same tender place. That letter had also touched a spot that had been hit before. It was still much too alive.

Shortly after I became a Christian there grew a desire to do something more vital for the Lord than just giving. At that particular time, Virginia and I had more income than we needed, and we were led to gift seven thousand dollars to a Christian work that seemed most worthy to us. Shortly thereafter, I was invited to spend a little time in its administration. Assistance was needed in overhauling procedures and help needed in bolstering the tottering finances.

It seemed like a wonderful opportunity to work directly with a well-regarded Christian organization, and it was exciting to anticipate working for a while in a Christian atmosphere. I had become increasingly weary of the salty language and loose moral behavior in many secular businesses. It was funny because I had never noticed these things before I became a Christian. Here was the chance to work for a few months in the holy climate of a Christian endeavor.

A few months later I staggered from the place with two painful lessons. First, I'd been shaken by my analysis revealing the portion of each dollar collected that ever got out to

the field! Then another big cloudburst—the leader's relationship with a staff member!

Being a new Christian, I began to observe some who named
the Name of Christ, but continued to live like the world. This
taught a stark lesson: that I must now endeavor to walk more
uprightly now that I am called a Christian.

(A Greek officer who repeatedly fell into trouble was finally
brought before his famous leader, Alexander the Great, who
said, "Soldier, what is your name?" The reply of the misbe-
having warrior shocked him. "Sir, my name is Alexander."

The great general's reply is apt for every Christian alive
today. Alexander the Great dismissed the troublemaker with
this warning: "Soldier, change your ways—or change your
name!")

We must remember that the world is constantly watching us
to see if we are any different, now. We are all living an epistle
—either an epistle exalting Christ's Name or debasing it with
our actions. In effect, we have CHRISTIAN stenciled across our
sweatshirts, and we must act accordingly. This applies to even
the smallest things like courtesy in driving, treatment toward
salesmen, police, and all others.

Much later, after my Clifton's Cafeteria baptism and after
Astro-Science, there was a short season between jobs when a
similar opportunity presented itself with another Christian
work. The needs were similar, and they felt that I was just the
man to help them for a bit. Enthusiasm for this promising
ministry again prompted us to invest since the spiritual potential was extraordinary.

You guessed it! Two months later, the evidence seemed
clear that there was a questionable relationship developing
between the married leader and an employee. I sensed an
urgency to counsel before it got out of hand—both for the sake
of the individuals and for the future of the ministry itself.
I fancied that I now had both the spiritual understanding

strength and the compassion to handle this delicate matter. It blew up with a roar!

Within days after my private exhortation to the leader, I was personally maligned, discredited, and reviled. "How dare I have such sordid thoughts!" The mate of the leader came close to physically assaulting me. And soon a letter was circulated among the membership coast-to-coast declaring that my bad management had wreaked havoc on the ministry. What was meant for good had been suddenly turned against me.

Thus my first two sorties had resulted in lightning striking twice! I had first handled both exhortations privately in accordance with the Scriptural procedure. That peace that passes all understanding became a *living reality* in the very midst of both of these difficult furnaces.

A few weeks later we flew off to Hawaii to lick our wounds, feeling that we needed to sort out both of these traumatic and humiliating experiences. The Lord had given us a promise from Isaiah 41 : 10, 11 which says, *Fear thou not; for I am with thee: be not dismayed; for I am thy God: I will strengthen thee; yea, I will help thee; yea, I will uphold thee with the right hand of my righteousness. Behold, all they that were incensed against thee shall be ashamed and confounded. . . .*

Virginia and I went to the little island of Kauai where we drove from Lihue to the most remote spot on the island. Way up at Kokee Park we stopped at the museum where we met its curator, a wonderful Christian lady. She graciously inquired where we lived. When we told her she said, "Oh, so you are from thus and so! Have you heard about the fraud that a businessman pulled on the poor blank organization?"

We almost fainted! Here we were 2,700 miles from home and the news of our "crime" had traveled before us!

I sucked in my breath and declared, "I am that man!"

She stammered, "Heavens, I'm sorry I ever said anything. Tell me your side of this story. I am sure there is more to it — you don't look like a bad person."

I replied, "The Lord has sealed our lips and if you have a need to know the facts please ask Him."

I had also been given another word from the Lord on this matter. He had shown us that I was now to focus my time on the Bible recording's ministry. He had said, "Read how Nehemiah was pressed to come down from My new assignment to rebuild the wall so as to defend himself. He refused to stop his new work, and I was his defense. If you now want to be your own explainer you can go ahead—but if you will trust Me I will do it in due time."

This proved to be a valid leading from the Lord, for without personally defending our action, God in His own time brought the facts to light in His own way. The Lord says that He will be our Defender and if we trust Him He will always prove it. It usually takes time and therein we must bridle our impatience. But He is never a minute too early or too late.

Satan works whenever he can to torment us into ill feeling toward certain of these members of God's family. It is vital that we not allow him access to plant his seeds of bitterness and discord among us.

God's children really are the salt of the earth. They're a lovely family and a few failures among its members in no way disproves this glorious truth. Then, too, I have also been careless in similar matters and have sinned thereby against other Christians.

Perhaps one more little example may be helpful. A young minister friend conveyed greetings, then told us of a need. His brother—a contractor—was in a temporary financial bind because his bank hadn't yet released certain construction impounds. This had jeopardized one of his brother's foremen.

"Could you loan $3,000 to my brother's foreman for just a week? This will strengthen my witness to the man, and my brother says he will stand behind your loan." The young minister explained how this loan would help his brother keep the foreman from leaving his construction company.

I agreed, "For a week, sure! No problem at all; glad to do it!"

Eleven days later, our $3,000 had left town for good! But now the brother, also a Christian businessman, just couldn't see why he should be involved with our problem. He hadn't gotten the money, had he? Another example of yielding to the temptation to fudge when later developments show that keeping a vow will be costly—just another "misunderstanding."

For twenty years I had just taken for granted the so-called big bad business world's integrity regarding its word. I had personally committed my companies for millions of dollars by an oral assent. Sometimes it would be a promise to buy thousands of dollars' worth of products or services from another firm. At other times it was an agreement to produce hard-to-estimate electronics at a fixed price—and all with just a handshake over a desk or dinner, sometimes in a foreign land. A hundred million dollars' worth of transactions are made daily on the Wall Street Stock Exchange floor by hand gestures. And they are kept—whether the deals proved good or disastrous by the close of the trading day.

Businessmen throughout the world know they *must* back these promises and commitments—regardless of the cost to them. They know that reneging on such a promise would finish them in their field. Those decisions on the Exchange floor must be made with such speed that the time needed to write up the deal would make the entire system unworkable. So the honor and the very life of a business house depends on its backing those oral and hand-signal transactions involving millions.

Somehow, the prince of this world seems to work overtime to try to foster his dirty tricks between Christians in this very realm. I have felt his force working this way in my own mind. There have been times, for example, when I would be reviewing the funds available to pay bills. The secular suppliers I knew wouldn't stand for lateness and then I would start rationalizing: "We must present a good stewardship testimony to these non-Christian suppliers. So perhaps I won't distribute our funds in strict accordance with the aging of the bills. Maybe we can let these Christian suppliers' bills go for another week."

This is *wrong!* Galatians 6:10 says, *As we have therefore opportunity, let us do good unto all men, especially unto them who are of the household of faith.* And I have had to ask the Lord more than once to forgive me for such shabby thinking!

Somehow, we seem vulnerable to treating our Christian brothers more poorly than we treat those of the world. I think the enemy tries to fog up our thinking in this area. Perhaps he tries to take advantage of the fact that a Christian won't sue another one—that he won't use strong-arm tactics on another —that he won't really get tough on another Christian brother or firm. But that is wrong motivation—and it is un-Scriptural.

Sometimes I think some even take subconscious advantage of the world's reluctance to crack down on a Christian enterprise. It is a reproach to the Lord's name that bankers sometimes hesitate to deal with churches for this very reason. Their experience hasn't always been as good with them as it ought to be. The elders of a church seem at times not to feel the same rending conviction when commitments for their church aren't met as they do in their personal affairs. And they wouldn't operate their own company this way—running late with bills, and keeping promises when convenient.

Then Satan also likes to throw Christians at other Christians. Have you ever noticed how much more you are wounded by the failures or harsh words of another Christian? I guess that we expect such things from the world and shrug them off without much pain; but let a Christian treat us poorly and our heart is broken! Yes, it really hurts—and Satan tries to make the most of this.

He tries to get us feeling that the majority of Christians are bad, and tries to graft in his patented roots of bitterness. Don't let him do it! He is the accuser of the brethren and the father of lies. David said in Psalm 55:12–14, *For it was not an enemy that reproached me; then I could have borne it; neither was it he that hated me that did magnify himself*

against me; then I would have hid myself from him: But was
thou, a man mine equal, my guide, and mine acquaintance.
We took sweet counsel together, and walked unto the house
of God in company.

Since half of my life has been spent in the business world,
I know how the non-Christian world functions. And now I
have lived through some years among the Lord's children.
I have watched them *both* in all manner of situations.

This is my testimony! God's children are truly the salt of
the earth. They are indeed wonderfully different in spite of
Satan's spotlights on our occasional stumblings. They are a
choice lot and I, for one, look forward with enthusiasm to an
eternity with my brothers and sisters in Christ! The lovely
Bride of a marvelous Bridegroom!

Yes, as I read the wounding letter, the sharp knuckle was
pounding again in that same old sensitive spot. I had flared
for a moment in frustration. I had discovered that one more
tantrum from that "old man" still lurked inside. Then suddenly
I realized—the $4,000 knuckle was ramming against the spot
all right, but surprised it wasn't hurting like it use to! I started
to talk to Him.

"Dear Lord, thank You for that knuckle. You tell us that we
are to give thanks in *everything* for this is the will of God.
I'm sorry it took so many years to deaden that unforgiving
'live' spot in my being. That ugly flaw in my spirit was *so
hard* for You to put to death, wasn't it? And forgive me, Lord,
for nearly allowing a root of bitterness to set in. I know that
You will somehow make up for this loss and the future of our
ministry doesn't depend on this income anyhow. It depends
only *on You*. Forgive me for looking to this source and not to
You—and forgive me for my fleshly reaction. And also for the
anger toward my dear brother. Lord, rekindle in me a new
and still deeper love for him. You tell us to forgive one another, even as God for Christ's sake has forgiven us. It's worth
the four thousand to know that sharp knuckle won't be needed

on me quite as much anymore. Keep it handy though; You will have to poke me in some of the other 'live' spots. I know You will somehow help us with that payroll money tomorrow. I love You for Your patience with me and for Your mercy. Amen."

The Lord is—on occasion—at work exposing more than one spiritual weak area in us at the same time. That's why we occasionally experience a series of problems all at once. Money is one of His greatest tools of Christian discipline and training. We seem sensitive and superalive in the realm of our pocketbook, so He wonderfully uses finances to teach, test and to develop us spiritually.

It's always so easy for us to talk about financial faith until the bills are past due. When money setbacks compound, we can then gauge the true quality of our faith. God often uses money to bless us in time of need, but also to regulate at times our comings and goings. Sometimes He lovingly withholds funds until He knows the time for us to make a certain move has fully come. It's no wonder Jesus had so much to say about money; He knew its value as a shaping tool for His vessels!

And as I reflected on my own life I was finally able to look back and see how these trials I had complained about at the time had been so essential to my spiritual development. The Bible says . . . *all have sinned and come short of the glory of God* (Romans 3:23). That sure fit me and I had picked up some valuable nuggets—some real treasures from my own life's valleys. A discovery that was High Adventure, too!

18

The Shaking Earth

As we leaped from bed, fragments from the shattered lamp snowed down and the fortress-thick house acted like flimsy mâché as she took the waves of energy released from the earth's undercrust miles down! The staccato force of fifty Hiroshima bombs was bucking and heaving our world. Gulps of water cascaded across the rose garden fifty feet from the pool.

Something gigantic was chewing blocks from the high surrounding fences! It disturbed our ninety-foot redwood and the rows of stately cypress as they whipped and danced in thirty-foot arcs to the deadly tune. The old place groaned and shrieked in agony while the marble table flew in obedience to the whipping forces!

By the time I had finished shouting, "Dear Father, in the Name of Jesus, help us!" Thirty seconds had already gone by. Several miles north and east sixty people had already passed from time into eternity as their broken bodies lay under tons of debris astride the Sylmar fault. Within fifty-eight seconds, a billion dollars in damage was strewn across the valley floor!

There was immediate and automatic prayer before the dawn and minutes later seven shapes converged in a hand-welded circle. We wanted to be together, and little five-year-old Heather was still quivering as the earth continued to liven our praises to the Lord.

Figurines and china from friends and faraway bazaars that had patiently stood pleading for loving glances now received them — for the last time. The beautiful oak floors lay speckled in color with sharp edges. Cabinets in the butler's pantry and kitchen had thrown open their arms to give out their cups and plates, saucers, and canned goods. It was a gingerly walk for those bare feet.

Through the drapes a forboding column of black smoke! A great fire had triggered in Granada Hills — in an instant. The click of light switches was futile and unanswered. Moving to the desk I hurried to phone our relatives, and also David over in Mission Hills. We knew this one had brought more trouble than anyone could ever handle — wherever it had been centered — but there was no way to know which way. The phone lines were dumb. "How about the radio?" But the stations were just as confused and curious and then I remembered, "Oh, no, Texas tonight!"

Yes, the Lord had been working out a number of things in us through that little series of misunderstandings. The healing in the money area had started and a new liberty was just dawning from the tentacles of mammon. The excessive dependence on substance had been mercifully dealt with by a loving Heavenly Father and we were feeling a deep peace.

Finally came the realization that my Lord really would supply my needs. No longer was there such a fight and struggle over business matters as though everything depended on me. He had finally gotten through to this hardhead that *He* wanted to be my *All* and my *supply*. At last, I could say, "What if Bible Voice is a struggle, and the electronics plant, too? What if we should have to move out of the big house some day? The Lord is with us and He will never forsake us," and finally I mean it!

It was exciting to sense this simple truth. To feel the liberty from "things." Not a dollar, not the factory, nor the house, will be needed in eternity anyhow.

During the prodding from that knuckle another area of Christian behavior was also being worked out by the Lord. The importance of keeping our *own word*, both in letter, and spirit.

He pointed to His Word about "vowing a vow" during the heartaches from the misunderstandings. The Bible says, *If a man vow a vow unto the Lord, or swear an oath to bind his soul with a bond; he shall not break his word, he shall do according to all that proceedeth out of his mouth* (Numbers 30:2). He was spotlighting the consequences from failure to live His Word in the hard nitty-gritty of life. And He was saying, "See how these failures by others to live My Word hurt you. Now see that you learn from this lesson how to treat others."

How comfortable it would be for us to be able to change that which we have vowed — later — after events reveal the difficulties in fulfilling the promise. Life is a continual chain of choices and commitments, and we are confronted with temptations to fudge a little on vows made.

I said, "I see it, Lord; and with Your help I'll try to live a testimony in this realm of vows regardless of cost. I'll be more prayerful about making promises and try to be more careful about going through with them. The problems we have experienced due to the failure of others proves that we must not do the same thing ourselves."

Be sure you mean what you say to God. He's listening and He may take you at your word. As He hears, He may test you!

But in the aftermath of the quake my thoughts jumped around like this: "Midland, Texas! Bill Mayne? Tonight? Texas International departure at 10:30 this morning! Oh, not today, not after this killer earthquake. Bill wouldn't expect me to. They wouldn't want me to leave my family *today*. I'll phone him. No, I forgot the phones are out; the quake must have collapsed a switching station somewhere. Oh well, maybe the airplanes won't be flying out of Los Angeles. It probably damaged the control tower or the GCA equipment.

"What was that You said, Lord? It's better not to vow! Oh, Lord, You aren't going to test me on this 'vow' lesson so soon are You? Surely, not with this kind of a crush!"

But the promise had been made, and my commitment written to Bill two months earlier. I could see his situation down there, even while the dust was settling around the house. Bill and his Christian businessmen had been advertising the meeting for four weeks, and they had already rented the Holiday Inn meeting hall. The posters were printed and hundreds of invitations mailed out. The prayer groups had spent hours on their knees for this meeting.

And now that the phone lines were down Bill couldn't be reached to even discuss a new arrangement. I saw it in my mind. Here it was—a quick test of the very truth God had just been speaking to me about.

"What would Jesus do in this situation?" I thought. That's a good thing to ask yourself in any situation. Jesus always did the will of the Father, and the Father's will is in His Word. The Word says we are to keep our vows. I knew that Jesus would go to Midland!

I shared the warfare that was going on inside of me with Virginia and the family. They weren't too sure just what I ought to do about the Texas meeting. Some of the house walls were down, lights out, and the basement looked ominous. There was fuel oil around the furnace and no phones. We still didn't know if Virginia's family, the Bible Voice staff, or our friends were safe. We didn't even know whether Bible Voice still existed over there in Van Nuys.

The radio was just giving early reports about a crack in the huge Van Norman Reservoir perched above our San Fernando Valley, but I sensed the Lord's mind on going. But what would our friends and Virginia's family think? What would my own family think? People could wonder why I'd leave this mess and fly off to the safety of Texas with only the excuse of one little meeting!

I threw some things into a suitcase and walked out leaving Virginia, the girls, and Don standing there in the middle of the debris. Just as I was pulling out of the driveway another big shock rattled the gates! My heart was heavy and my mind full of colliding thoughts as I started toward the office.

But praise God! It was a fantastic miracle. The Bible Voice facilities are on the Van Nuys Airport, a couple of miles still closer to the quake epicenter, yet not a thing had been harmed. Not a desk, duplicator, amplifier, or even a recorder had been smashed. There was just one little mountain of tapes in the production area to be put back on shelves. Incredible! "Thank You, dear Lord."

Now it was 10:01 as Charles Rand drove me toward International Airport. I could see the Hughes Hangar just as the car radio crackled out the news: "Attention! Evacuate immediately! Everyone must evacuate from the Van Norman Dam southward to the Ventura Boulevard. From Sepulveda to Corbin Avenue — water is seeping through the dam wall at a hundred gallons per minute. The dam may not hold if the aftershocks continue."

I started to pray, "Oh, dear Lord, please help Virginia!" (Young George had taken her Firebird to check on his girl friend's family out in Sylmar.) I went on, "Virginia doesn't have a phone, no electricity, no help, and now no car. If that reservoir breaks, it will take Bible Voice and the house, too, and I wonder if our Bible Voice people heard that report? The announcer said the police are driving through every street with loud speakers, so I guess they'll be safe."

I started to talk to the Lord again and felt certain now that the situation had changed so drastically that He would agree with me.

"Dear Heavenly Father, thank You for Your mercy to us to-day. Not a hair of our head has been touched. Bible Voice must have been protected by Your ministering angels, too. The old house is standing, and I think it can be fixed. Thank You for preventing fire in our oil furnace.

"Now I especially want to thank You for alerting me to this serious threat of the wipeout of both Bible Voice and our house from the dam problem. I feel that it's my duty to go back. We must protect the master recordings of the Bible and the computer tapes and there's real danger to my family. Dear Father, in the Name of Jesus, I must have a word from You now! Can I turn around and meet my responsibilities in this fractured place?"

We were in Inglewood now and I could see the airport sign ahead. But I thought we could just drive off the freeway at Century and head back on the opposite ramp.

Then it came again. "It's better not to vow a vow . . . ! If you will go on to Texas and take care of My business, you can trust Me to take care of your business here. I want you to minister in Texas, tonight. Continue!"

It was illogical and unnatural, but it seemed supernatural! I had finally learned by now that His ways really are above our ways!

I tried to phone Virginia from the Airport again and again, but nothing was operating that morning. I shuffled onto the DC-9 and we were soon airborne, heading East. With help from the concordance I started to thumb my Bible, rereading the Scriptures about earthquakes.

It was especially thrilling on that flight to read how *earthquakes in divers places* (Mark 13:8) is one of Jesus' signposts, that we may know when we are in the "last days." It was also exciting to read about one *particular earthquake* — and I longed for that one as we cruised at 32,000 feet!

After the last climactic battle plays out on the Plains of Armageddon, Christ Himself descends upon Mount Olivet.

Then comes the shaking of the earth and rocks groaning as the mountain splits and a crystal river bursts forth—first in one direction and then the other! It waters the thirsty plains and the desert blooms burst forth. Thus is ushered in that thousand years; Eden restored! The Millennium Glory! What a wonderful earthquake!

The Lord allowed me just four minutes to talk about quakes that night. The place was jammed with Texans. The steps along the back were carpeted with young people and even the chairs on the platform were used. Their prayers had done the job—the people were out in extraordinary numbers. Those wonderful Texans really meant business with God that night! Four minutes of earthquake talk, and fifty-six minutes about Redeemer, Messiah, Dayspring, Healer, Counselor, Lily of the Valley, and Bright and Morning Star.

And the very night of the Shaking Earth, twenty-seven made Him Lord. About the same number (or a few less) met Him as Baptizer with the Holy Spirit. A few hearts were mended, and some felt His healing touch.

Then I knew—and He won't have to speak this one to me again! He had dramatically underscored his lesson about the keeping of a vow. He had done His work in my own heart there, too—deep in the heart of Texas!

A few days later, I learned something fascinating about the dam. God's hand had stayed the most serious tragedy this nation would have ever experienced. Eighty-thousand people live below in the path of the huge lake.

Robert Noel, a Christian maintenance engineer at the dam, raced up its earthen slope that morning. He had run from his house below within seconds of the mind-stupefying jolt. Bob knew the corner of the face that hadn't yet been reinforced. He was fighting for breath as he squinted in the dawn light out across the water. It was now 6:10 A.M.

Bob was shocked to see their big catwalk bent like a toy erector set and the towers completely gone. Then his eyes fell on the awful gouge from an earthslide that had thinned the inside of the wall itself! The waters lapped restlessly at the edge of the new cracks. The thick concrete inner facing of the dam was grotesque—like a brittle sheet of ice cracked by a heavy boot. Noel prayed as he thought of the thousands below and urgently cried out to God for help! Suddenly Bob Noel started to sing of the mercies of the Lord when he again looked at that water sloshing at the cracks. He had remembered in that moment some of their frustrating troubles of past months at Van Norman Reservoir.

The water for the big holding lake for the City of Los Angeles had been cut off on July 7, 1970, from its old Colorado river supply. That water was overly expensive since it had to be pumped at considerable cost up and over the mountain ranges. An eastern Sierra slope aqueduct was operating, and now a second new one from the High Sierras was ready, but it developed trouble when a barrel fractured.

A management decision was made to let the level drop a little since that broken barrel from the new aqueduct would be flowing again any day now. The wonderful syphon effect that the engineers had conceived for bringing the water through the new aqueduct from the north would flow without those big, expensive pumps that had been used on the Colorado river supply.

Then trouble continued to hound completion of that new barrel. Now water level at the lake had fallen from a high of 1,117 feet down to 1,112 feet. Not too much need to worry about yet since the problem would be fixed any day. Then it happened! About seven days before that awful Tuesday the winds shifted, and the Santa Ana desert winds began to blow across the city. Those strange hot desert winds commenced to dry everything in their path.

People below started to drain the huge reservoir alarmingly. All across the big valley, hundreds of thousands of lawn sprinklers started to spray. Trouble at the Van Norman Reservoir! Soon they would again have to valve in that expensive old Colorado water supply to bring the water in the lake back up. But the level at Van Norman plummeted!

The all-knowing Lord of Heaven who had foreseen the killer quake had in His own intricate way brought that water level clear down to *1,109.30 feet*. Almost to the inch mark on that broken dam face!

Thousands of other reports flew over the next days. Some were frightening about situations experienced at that brain-jarring moment; but I think the funniest was a line from my sister who was sleeping in our guest bedroom that morning.

Helen was visiting California for her first time. She had been seriously distraught and nervous over recent months, and friends in Ohio thought the visit might bring relief from her despondency since she lost her husband. Helen had come with another of my sisters. Ruth had to get back to Michigan and she had left two days before, right according to their original trip plan.

Helen was progressing beautifully from her own participation in the Christian meetings and the fellowship in California. She had responded to an invitation at a Palm Springs church and had given her heart to Christ two days earlier. So at the last minute, Helen decided to stay in California for an extra week.

At 6:01 the tall grandfather clock banged across the foot of Helen's bed as the furniture stirred around her room erratically! Within two minutes as the family met together downstairs, Helen walked bright-eyed toward us saying, "Oh, I'm so glad I didn't go back with Ruth. Just think—I might have missed all this!"

We praised the Lord in our hearts, and knew that Jesus really had healed Helen.

19

Visit With a King

Little grains of sand by the thousands seemed to be floating across the road and out over the ripples on the desert floor. It was sunny and pleasant as we entered Palm Springs — except for that wind! But it quieted as we parked in front of the big Riviera Hotel auditorium.

The Full Gospel Business Men's Convention had already been underway a day or two. It was a long trip down here for just one day, but neither of us could stay. Harald and I were to be the speakers for their special women's banquet.

I had been asked to pinch-hit for a famous lady who had been the announced speaker, and I knew the women would be disappointed! "It's an awkward spot," I thought as I scanned the big room full of ladies chattering over their plates. "Boy, they can fill a room full of sound, but they are a mighty handsome group of women!" "Just to look at them it could have been a meeting of the High Society 400!" (I had long since discovered that the Christians aren't just the salt of the earth, spiritually. After becoming a Christian I had been delightfully surprised to discover His kids are some of the best looking, most vibrant people on earth!)

Just before the introduction, Herbert Ellingwood was ushered to the platform and there was a buzzing of voices all around me. This was my first chance to meet Herb, who is the legal affairs secretary to the governor. They asked him to greet the gathering, and it was then that Harald and I first learned of the arrangements for us to visit the governor.

Two days later, Harald, Pat, Shirley and I were alternately sharing, planning, and praying as we cruised north on the jet. Richard was moving around peering at us from odd angles and clicking his camera. (Richard Dalrymple is the religious writer on the big Los Angeles evening newspaper, The *Herald-Examiner*.) Harald had met Richard down at Palm Springs where Richard had been covering the convention for his paper. Now Richard was along with us to cover Pat's afternoon meeting in the capital.

There were only a few empty seats left in the big Civic Auditorium as 4,700 clapped and clapped while Pat sparkled and moved them with his message. Then he motioned to Shirley! She stood before the mike with Pat's arm around her and started to testify. I had never experienced anything quite like this!

I still can't remember what Shirley said in those first few minutes while we could still understand her. Gradually tears came to her eyes, and she began to weep while she spoke. It seemed to come from the depths of her soul and the people began to move with the same spirit that was stirring within her own heart. Shirley was talking and sobbing about her love for Jesus. There was hardly a word anyone could make out, but it communicated beyond mere words. The formal program was finally over and then a quiet invitation was given. More than two hundred streamed behind the big stage area to surrender their lives to Christ.

Herb Ellingwood had everything prewired. An advancing wedge cleared a path for us through the forest of outstretched hands and bright faces as we moved out to the waiting limousine.

Finally its doors could be closed and we rolled slowly out into the street toward the mansion. Herb glanced at his watch as we walked past the guard gate and up the long sidewalk to the door, "Perfect — we're right on time."

When Herb had made the announcement of our visit in Palm Springs, he shook his head in wonder as he told of the incredible schedule that the governor was on. It wasn't only the hundred matters of government he must cope with in the capitol. The governor was right then in the heat of his reelection campaign, so it wasn't just the hours, but the minutes, too, that must be computer-scheduled to manage his enormous responsibilities. Over the past week, evening prayer had gone up from Herb and a few of his close friends. Miraculously some time had opened up with the governor and his wife. And now here we were!

It was late Sunday afternoon and security officers manned both of the guard houses in the front and rear, but it seemed as gracious and informal as if we had just walked into Mr. Jones' lovely home down the street.

What a handsome pair! He moved to the pantry quickly and served us soft drinks himself. ("Now that's *classy* service!" I thought.)

There was a few minutes of shop talk between the longtime friends who had each spent considerable time in the same industry. The names of both are very big in the field! and in a way, they were now both stars again in chosen new fields. Then it started!

It was a hundred minutes of concentrated lightning! As we sat in an irregular square lounging easily in the bright room, the talk shifted and leaped. Moving gently and then with intensity about this and that — on and on it went! So much was covered in only a hundred minutes, yet there was hardly a segment after the first ten minutes that didn't bear on the Lord. The Bible was being interpreted by different ones in the light of all of the explosive contemporary events!

During that afternoon the governor delighted all of us with his deep knowledge and fascination with the prophetic Scriptures. The precious minutes flew as one after another would relate the ancient Bible prophecies now being fulfilled — the same problems that the governor faces daily as he leads the twenty million within his own responsibility.

I volunteered that by the Lord's definition he was like a "king" and that God says He raises up and pulls down kings Himself; and how the governor's responsibilities exceed those of King Agrippa of the New Testament to whom Paul so eloquently testified. That king, we speculated, had fewer than a million to govern while the governor now had the awesome responsibility for twenty times that many. Both of these arrows of truth seemed to strike target, and he nodded his head slowly.

(On the way home from that unique cottage meeting we agreed that God had blessed the state by raising up a high calibre of man to lead it in such a difficult hour. We got a new sense of his integrity and his boldness to lead, under God.)

He has a rare willingness to govern as his conscience dictates, and he did not impress us as one to falter in sensitive decisions just to be a people pleaser! We had encouraged him from the Word to move under the inspiration of God's wisdom daily and to make decisions in harmony with God's Word. The Bible says no man can pull him from his appointed seat until it is God's own time. We also reminded him that the Lord would likewise be involved with the next occupant of the White House. God says He watches over nations and that His hand is in their affairs. They can operate only within His permissive limits. That afternoon we all recalled God's ultimate dealings with the Caesars and the Roman Empire, and the Hitlers. He does have His limits with evil nations too!

Our last fifteen minutes at the governor's mansion seemed to pivot around the Scripture theme *in the last . . . days I will pour out of my Spirit upon all flesh . . .* (Acts 2:17). Short testimonies and stories commenced to pour from the lips of one after another sketching in the picture of its fulfillment in our day.

The Boones wrote on the flyleaf of their new book as they handed it to the pair: "Please read *A New Song* when you have time. We want you to know how a few drops of this new rain of God have fallen at our house, too." Then the governor took a copy of the book *The Solution to Crisis-America* and expressed surprise and pleasure as we told him about the thousands now praying for him daily throughout his State.

The doorbell rang! Herb was back, pointing at his watch. "The computer was flashing its light."

It was as though we all wanted to go on, but instead we got up and milled around for a few seconds shaking hands. Harald said, "Before we leave I think we ought to pray for the governor." Then someone else suggested, "Why don't we hold hands." There was a little backing and shuffling to find a hand while we formed a circle. The governor happened to be moving between Herb and myself right then and wheeling he reached for our hands.

It grew quiet; the circle was full of V.I.P.'s. We waited — my feet shuffled a little. Who would pray? Maybe Pat or Harald, or maybe Herb — everyone outranked me. The governor was on that tight schedule, I remembered, and it seemed like too many seconds had gone by already. Awkwardly, I cleared my throat and as the first words cleared my lips — it hit me! It would have happened to anyone in that circle — anyone who would have started to pray!

The power of God shot through me and formed the prayer and moved physically on me — and at once! My hands began to tremble slightly from the presence of the Lord. I had felt it a few times before. It would occasionally happen when I was laying hands on someone for prayer, but *this* was no place for that sort of thing! Not when you're holding hands with a governor! While the prayer flowed, I was telling my hands to behave. Always before, when I felt this power of God physically, I had been able to discipline it. When it happened when I was praying for someone unfamiliar with it that I thought might be disturbed, I would curb it. But now with all my strength I moved upon that right arm to hold it in check. It was beyond my strength to control the pulsating.

We were finished now and all the hands dropped. The quiet good-byes were mouthed. And I was more than a little concerned and embarrassed until I caught the governor's eye. He seemed to be looking at me with a half-question and half-tenderness in his face. It had been some kind of a visit!

Now we were moving through the street again in the black limousine as we rolled by manicured lawns and large homes. Small chatterings of delight; "Wasn't it good that we were able to share with them about this and that?" "Aren't they great!" "She seemed so happy to have us, didn't she?" "You'd think they didn't have anything else to do but spend the afternoon with us!"

Then Herb interrupted, "Say, I must share something wonderful with you and I still can hardly believe it. Do you know what happened toward the end in our prayer circle? I had the governor's hand, and it commenced to pulsate when George started, and then it continued until the prayer was over."

"Good night!" I said. "The power of God seemed to come down on me and it must have flowed right through the governor on into Herb's hand." I told them what had happened to me and how I had fought to control it. We agreed that this sign from the Lord had some special significance for the governor. Just what we weren't sure, but we were certain that God would not waste such a remarkable manifestation unless the governor was very special to Him.

The next morning in the capitol after returning from a breakfast meeting with the lieutenant governor, we met with Richard Dalrymple, the newspaperman. Richard had been stirred by the fellowship that we had all enjoyed on this trip. Somehow this, plus Harald's work with him back in Palm Springs, had begun to take root way down inside him. Richard wanted us to pray with him for the Baptism with the Holy Spirit when we got back from the meeting with the lieutenant governor.

We all walked over to our motel room, but we didn't get very far with our instruction to him until we sensed that Richard, the religious writer for the great Hearst paper, hadn't yet met Jesus as his Saviour. And we told him how he must first be saved before praying for the baptism. Within the hour, Richard had established harmony with his Lord. Richard accepted Christ as his Saviour and was born again about mid-day right there in the motel room in the capital city.

We then made a date with him for later that week. Richard and his wife came over to our house the following Thursday evening. Both Richard and Sandra had gotten messed up in recent years by dabbling with many kinds of religious experiences: Yoga, transcendental meditation, Buddhism, and varieties of eastern religions. We spent several hours with our Bibles open, and then he and Sandra renounced Satan and all this with their own lips. They asked God's forgiveness for their spiritual carelessness. And now we felt it was time!

Both Richard and Sandra left our house that night baptized with the Holy Spirit. They were chattering, glowing, and hugging each other as they moved down the winding front walk toward their car.

Now there are at least two of them: McCandlish Phillips on the *New York Times* and Richard Dalrymple of the *Herald Examiner* on the West Coast. Now there were two reporters on major newspapers aflame for Jesus and in positions to communicate to millions.

It was along about then, as I remember, that several things began to turn over in my mind. I began to suspect part of the *why* of "Mister Boone." I began to sense that our Lord may have planned it this way. Fashioning Pat with all of his unusual variety of attributes, it seemed as though a loving God had arranged favor with men for Pat, and I began to suspect that Pat had been raised up for such a time as this.

There is an urgent need for a fresh voice in this hour. Suddenly I remembered how Pat—without effort—has the attention of so many people and the key to so many doors! I couldn't recall another personality in all history—known to so many millions of people—who had stood to proclaim, "Jesus is my Lord and He also has baptized me with His Spirit."

But since the Lord hasn't repented of His gift of free will, I knew it would be now up to the young man alone to decide what he would do with his awesome spiritual opportunity.

And I rejoiced as I realized, "Here I am—*writing*. Everyone of us is a living epistle and all of us are, in a sense, writing with our lives. That part of the Epistle of George Otis that has been written by his own strength and talent will prove to be just wood, hay, stubble—phony, dull and dangerous."

Yet, increasingly, I trust, George is finally learning to let Jesus write a little through his life so that *he which hath begun a good work . . . will perform it until the day of Jesus Christ* (Philippians 1:6). And so, whatever may be of value, whatever is lasting of it, whatever is true, is by God's hand alone.

Now I realize that my own epistle will never end. Choice by choice, chapter by chapter, on and on it will go. The restless boy, broken and grotesque with sin, is slowly being remolded as he skips along toward eternity, his hand in that of his beloved Christ Jesus.

It's *High Adventure* moving from time into eternity toward the place Christ has prepared for them that love Him.

The bell is ringing. It's that phone again! What next . . . ?